E D U C A T E D
G U E S S

A School Board Member Reflects

Howard Good

A SCARECROWEDUCATION BOOK

The Scarecrow Press, Inc.
Lanham, Maryland, and Oxford
2003

K H

A SCARECROWEDUCATION BOOK

Published in the United States of America
by Scarecrow Press, Inc.
A Member of the Rowman & Littlefield Publishing Group
4501 Forbes Boulevard, Suite 200, Lanham, Maryland 20706
www.scaroweducation.com

PO Box 317
Oxford
OX2 9RU, UK

British Library Cataloguing in Publication Information Available

Library of Congress Cataloging-in-Publication Data

Good, Howard, 1951–
  Educated guess : a school board member reflects / Howard Good.
    p. cm.
  "A ScarecrowEducation book."
  ISBN 0-8108-4759-0 (pbk. : alk. paper)
  1. Education—Aims and objectives—United States. 2. School boards—United States. I. Title.
LA217.2.G66 2003
370'.973—dc21

                                                              2003001299

∞™ The paper used in this publication meets the minimum requirements of American National Standard for Information Sciences—Permanence of Paper for Printed Library Materials, ANSI/NISO Z39.48-1992.
Manufactured in the United States of America.

10|25|04

To Joanne Loewenthal,
a school superintendent who really is super

CONTENTS

PART II   HONEY AND ASHES

FOREWORD

One of the first things I discovered about Howard Good is that he is a keen observer of human nature and a terrific storyteller. He is also the type of person I would want to serve on my school board—candid, funny, maybe a bit cynical, tough but fair, and filled with a passion for doing what makes practical sense. These attributes are essential for school board service.

Anyone who has served on a school board has stories to tell, but few have chronicled their experiences as Howard has here in *Educated Guess: A School Board Member Reflects*. Part reminiscence, part instructional guide, savvy school board veterans and anxious rookies alike will identify with Howard's wide-ranging tales of board service that "never ceased to seem an honor and privilege . . . though it quickly became a burden and curse as well."

Although Howard is both a school board president and journalism professor, his style is more like a coach. Each essay provides guidance to those facing common school board issues: school violence, censorship, public speaking, budget cuts, citizen complaints, internal conflicts, and the negative image that seems to dog school boards no matter what they do. To me, Howard's advice is right on: Assemble a group of inspired, mentally tough people who are conditioned to overcome adversity on their way to achieving their shared goals.

This book is filled with the insights that Howard has learned as a school board member for the past six years and as a teacher for many more. His references to history, popular culture, the collective wisdom of his board colleagues, and his own personal experiences put in context a sound philosophy for "guiding a school board through the murk of human decision making." Read and learn from this book. I appreciate the opportunity to lend my enthusiasm and support for this project.

Timothy G. Kremer
Executive Director
New York State School Boards Association

PREFACE

Six years ago I was elected to my local school board. I didn't undertake board membership as a literary experiment—in fact, sometimes it's hard to remember exactly why I did undertake it. But almost immediately after my election, I began writing the essays collected here. Who would've guessed that the other board members and the people who come to board meetings to whine, beg, criticize, or report would end up serving as my muses? Certainly not them. I'm still a little appalled by it myself.

The essays concern either one of two subjects: board membership or teaching. My membership on the school board has never ceased to seem an honor and a privilege to me, though it quickly became a burden and a curse as well. It's been a long time since I've been able to go anywhere in town, from the supermarket to the soccer field to a summer concert in the park, without running the risk of parents descending on me like a bunch of crazed bikers about to stomp somebody. Probably half the essays in this book are rooted in my contradictory feelings about board membership—the sense that it may be a necessary job, but it's also a damn frustrating one.

An almost equal number of essays deal with teaching. In some chapters I remember teachers I had, both good and bad. In others, I reflect on my own teaching (I've been a journalism professor for twenty years now). Educational reformers and researchers are forever proposing new ways (or old ways under catchy new names) to improve student performance. But a district can pursue "teaming," "looping," or a dozen other school reforms, and student performance will still lag if the teacher in the classroom—Mr. Bluni or Mrs. Miller or Miss Dolan—isn't any good. And what makes a good teacher? I would contend that it is the capacity to nurture and inspire students. There are a great many problems with American public education, including unfunded state and federal mandates, racial gaps in academic achievement, and overtesting, but perhaps the most fundamental and far-reaching dilemma is the lack of teachers who care, truly care, about the kids sitting right in front of them.

This book isn't going to win any awards for profundity, as I suspect the somewhat sappy previous sentence shows. Yet readers who saw some of these essays when they originally appeared in *Education Week, Teacher Magazine,* or *American School Board Journal* weren't unaffected by them. Occasionally, one would be so moved—my euphemism for "pissed off"—by something I wrote that he or she wouldn't even bother with a letter to the editor, but would e-mail his or her challenges and objections directly to me. Rather than being depressed by this, I was uplifted, for I believe, along with Dr. Johnson, that the worst thing you can do to a writer is ignore him. Or, to turn it around, the worst thing you can do to a reader is to let him be. I'll try not to let you be.

I

SCHOOL BOARD BLUES

SAY WHAT?

I'm perhaps more sensitive than most people to jargon. I have spent a large part of my working life, first as a journalist and now as a journalism professor and author, trying to avoid speaking or writing it. My models have been George Orwell, Red Smith (who quit *Sports Illustrated* because copy editors kept inserting the word "moreover" into his stories), and the King James version of the Bible.

Of course, journalism, like any other trade or profession today, has its own jargon. But as jargon goes, journalism's is refreshingly blunt. You slug a story and kill a graf. Nowhere does it approach the capacity of educational jargon to obscure the obvious. And I should know. I serve on a board of education.

When I was still just a regular taxpayer, I would sit in the audience at school board meetings and try to follow the discussion, but would soon catch myself contemplating the mole on the board president's face. I would feel guilty about having allowed my attention to wander. Now I realize that the meetings were conducted in a language designed precisely to make you focus on something else, anything else, even a hairy mole.

It is a language with all the melodiousness of the dry heaves. One of its chief characteristics is the use of unfamiliar, scientific-sounding abbreviations. School administrators can hardly speak without referring to

IEP, ERB, DLT, ISS, SCE, or RCT. After sufficient exposure to this kind of speech, the average person may feel a need for CPR.

Educational jargon also consists of what I call "noun-droids"—three or more nouns that have been wired together to form big, imposing, but ultimately inhuman phrases. I can open my vinyl binder labeled "School Board Workbook" to almost any page and find blood-curdling examples from "Tri-State Assessment Model Reference Card" to "teacher alternative compensation pilot." All those nouns in a row seem to suggest solidity and order, but they rarely denote or describe anything tangible. They mostly serve as camouflage for a lack of real activity. With just nouns and no verbs, the mind can't leap or grope or dream.

And then there are the buzzwords. "Evaluation" is one. "Model" is another. "Indicators" is a third. Put them all together, as in "value-added evaluation model key indicators," and you have the local patois, as well as the winner in an ugly language contest.

I hold the schools of education at colleges and universities across the country responsible for most of this verbal sludge. It seems you can't graduate from one of them as a certified teacher unless you can add the suffix "based" to at least five hundred words. Thus we have site-based councils and performance-based assessments and computer-based learning. What's next? Desk-based students?

Recently I got a particularly heavy dose of educational jargon when, as part of my board responsibilities, I went through a batch of job applications from prospective teachers. Applicants had been asked to write a brief statement about their experience and abilities. Once they ran out of jargon—ready-made phrases like "full potential," "least restrictive environment," "self-esteem"—they were lost. None was more lost than the young woman who applied for a job as a gym teacher. "It is very important for society," she wrote with a dictionary far from her elbow, "to emphasize lifelong physical activity instead of a sedimentary lifestyle."

Speaking of sediment, Orwell had an absolute abhorrence of muddy language. In his classic 1948 essay "Politics and the English Language," he argued that muddy language produces muddy thinking as often as the other way around. If we clarify our language, he said, we can clarify our thinking, and thinking clearly about the state of the world is a prerequisite for change. Orwell proposed that we improve the world by beginning, as he put it, "at the verbal end."

American public schools are under huge pressure today to improve. Politicians, parents, and taxpayer groups are calling for our students to perform better, both straight up and in comparison with students from Western Europe and Japan. But improving academic performance isn't simply a matter of raising standards. It costs money. It takes stamina. It antagonizes all the secret allies of the status quo.

There are more of these, and they are more powerful than you may realize. School boards, schools of education, teachers' unions, and teachers themselves are all accustomed to and invested in things as they are. The current system, whatever its failures, provides school board candidates with fat issues, schools of education with fat enrollments, and teachers' unions with fat asses.

Anyway, reform is hard work. It is easier to elaborate language, to add layers of jargon, to paint over problems with bureaucratese. So-called "stakeholders" on so-called "building-level teams" utilizing so-called "shared decision making" as outlined in the so-called "Plan to Plan" implement so-called "heterogeneous groupings." By which point, a mere parent hasn't the slightest clue what the so-called "hell" is going on.

If there is an air of menace about educational jargon, it is because, like all jargon, it is intended to scare off intruders—or, more precisely, to designate all people without the proper vocabulary as intruders. The result has been a steady decrease in public understanding and a steady increase in public hostility. How can the public feel anything but hostile toward something ominously labeled "criterion-referenced assessments" or "the performance-based process"?

We should turn these long, vague phrases back into simple action verbs. We should train teachers and school administrators to speak so that they can be understood. We should communicate with each other as with the stars.

But until that happens, perhaps everyone should just shut up.

2

THEN AND NOW

A few months after I was elected to the school board, a friend gave me as a belated congratulations gift a dusty old book she found at a library fair. The book was *The Challenge of School Board Membership* by Daniel R. Davies, a professor at Teachers College, Columbia University, and Fred W. Hosler, superintendent of schools in Oklahoma City. Originally published in 1949 (two years before I was born), the book proved popular enough to go through four printings by 1954.

My friend figured I would be amused by the differences between school board membership then and now, and she was right. The book was written at a time when better schools boasted not only a school psychologist, but also a school dentist; when the median expenditure per pupil was $99 a year; when authors could still describe education as "the seed-bed of democracy" without being accused of naïveté or political incorrectness.

Yet the book wasn't merely an amusing relic of a simpler age. I learned some facts from it; for example, school boards evolved out of special school committees set up by New England town meetings after school matters became too complex and demanding to be handled by the town meetings themselves. Even more important, I learned that despite the passage of fifty years, the basic operation of a school board really hasn't changed that much.

I'm not sure whether that is comforting or scary.

Davies and Hosler wrote that the proper functions of a board are policymaking (charting a course for the local school system) and evaluating (checking from time to time on how matters are progressing). But they also pointed out that boards frequently get sidetracked, bogged down, distracted—"become lost in a merry-go-round of administrative chores that are not properly theirs at all." Any board member who has sat through a meeting in which the district phone bill or the grade of gravel for the high school parking lot was discussed ad nauseam (and what board member hasn't?) knows exactly what the authors meant.

There is much else in *The Challenge of School Board Membership* that sounds depressingly familiar. For example, Davies and Hosler noted that less than 5 percent of the typical school budget went for books, paper, crayons, and other instructional supplies, while about 70 percent went for teachers' and principals' salaries. "It just does not make sense," they wrote, "to let the tail wag the dog."

Half a century later, it still doesn't make sense, but it is still happening. The latest figures from the Educational Research Service show that expenditures for books and materials are now less than 3 percent of the typical school budget. My own district hasn't enough money to buy science books for all eighth-graders, and yet our teachers are among the highest paid in the county. A complex combination of factors—state law, union contracts, school funding formulas—has seemingly rendered school boards powerless to fix such obvious imbalances.

One of the refreshing things about *The Challenge of School Board Membership* is that it treats all issues as ultimately resolvable. In 1949, the educational bureaucracy hadn't reached the Kafka-esque proportions it would in later years, and the book exhibits a sweet faith that even the toughest problems can be made to yield to practical reason and hard work. The very titles of its ten short chapters reflect this essential optimism, my hands-down favorite being "The Right Amount of Money and How to Get It."

But, of course, not every issue could be resolved, and boards still wrestle with many of the same problems Davies and Hosler spotlighted: inadequate budgets, crumbling school buildings, uninspired teachers, and overcrowded classrooms. If there is a real difference between school board service then and now, it isn't that today's boards face drastically different problems. It is that they face them with less confidence.

That is why the authors' observations remain pertinent. Their book contains a kind of moral vision of what school boards should do and how they should do it, expressed simply, directly, and without any of the jargon and cant that disfigure current educational writing.

The vision is child-focused. A board member, Davies and Hosler say, "is paid the highest compliment that parents can bestow—to him they entrust the welfare of their children. It is not a job to be taken lightly."

This is something board members need to hear, especially since so many have a tendency to micromanage and be drawn into side issues. Board members need to be reminded that the main reason they meet isn't to map school bus routes or conduct petty political feuds but to help ensure a good education for all children.

The authors offer a number of suggestions for board members. With some adjustments for gender-biased language, their advice makes as much sense today as it did in the late 1940s and early 1950s. Among the suggestions:

1. Keep in close, systematic touch with the community on educational policy: "The groups that shout the loudest do not necessarily represent the wishes of the majority."
2. Recognize the important role that school buildings and grounds have in the educational program: "If children are to grow into adults more sensitive to the beauty which surrounds them, they must experience beauty in the environment in which they spend so much time during the day—the school and its grounds."
3. Establish personnel policies that encourage the development of a good school staff: "The real difference between good and poor schools appears to be the quality of the people employed."
4. Learn to work effectively with the superintendent: "The basic division of labor principle . . . is that the board *legislates* and *evaluates* and the superintendent *executes*."
5. Be aggressive in helping finance the needs of the school system: "It is not education, it is failure to educate that is expensive."

Incidentally, Davies and Hosler saw little reason for marathon board meetings. "There is something wrong," they asserted, "when boards meet two or more times a month and the meetings last from 8 or 8:30 P.M. until midnight or after." They suggested solving the problem by getting better organized and not, as my board has done, by starting earlier in the evening.

What some consider a major weakness of school boards—that they are directed by well-meaning amateurs—Davies and Hosler considered a major strength. Nowhere else in the world, they wrote, is the control of education so close to the people. I don't think it is an exaggeration to say that today, when bureaucratic rules are proliferating and far-off, highly centralized corporations control many areas of our lives, the local school board is one of the few remaining examples of grassroots democracy.

The people I represent know me firsthand. If they have concerns, they can call me on the phone or stop by my house—and they do. This sometimes gets annoying, but it is an essential part of serving on a school board. We can only hope that fifty years and a thousand educational reforms from now, parents will still be able to interrupt a board member's supper.

3

SHADOW OF THE GUN

I'm fifty years old, a grizzled veteran of life's many battles, but I cried when I saw the dreadful scenes from the latest school shooting on TV. I cried because defenseless boys and girls had once more been cruelly gunned down. I cried because I could imagine the panic of parents whose children were caught in the chaos. I cried because no place in America is immune anymore—not churches or day care centers or schools—from the plague of violence.

In fact, with each new shooting, we seem to move tragically closer to a numb acceptance of murderous violence as a fixture of twenty-first-century public education. Not long ago, people, hearing about a school shooting, would say, or at least think, "It can't happen here." Few say or think that now. Most realize that it can happen anywhere. From California to Georgia, from the rural hinterlands to upscale suburbs, one all-American community after another has suffered the horror of gunfire on school grounds.

As a society, our response to the shootings has been woefully inadequate. If a mysterious disease were regularly striking down groups of children, would we remain so passive? Would we spare any effort to understand the cause? Would we rest until we found a cure? School violence is a disease, a raging fever, and yet we seem strangely unable to focus on curing it.

You don't need to remind me that districts have tightened security in their buildings or that states have begun to require schools to draw up safety plans. Santana High School in Santee, California, had a safety plan in place and security guards on premises, but that didn't prevent a student from opening fire there with a .22-caliber pistol, killing two and wounding thirteen. The surge in school violence is a bigger and more complex problem than any combination of surveillance cameras, metal detectors, security guards, bomb-sniffing dogs, and safety plans can solve.

Nor do the media help much either. News coverage of school shootings, particularly on TV, may even compound the problem. The kind of relentless, sensational, over-the-top coverage that greets the shootings lends a dark glamour to student violence, a celebrity aura that encourages copycats. Within a day of the shooting in Santee, violence threatened or actually erupted at a dozen schools across the country.

The media drive chilling images of school shootings deep into our consciousness—images of fleeing students, anxious parents, baby-faced killers in prison jumpsuits. What the media don't do is clarify the underlying issues. Is easy access to guns the source of the problem? Are violent movies and video games a contributing factor? After every shooting, we are treated by the media to the same old tired debate between gun-control advocates and opponents, or between critics of entertainment violence and its Hollywood defenders. They talk in clichés, and we half-listen, and then it is time for a commercial. Meanwhile, children go on killing other children.

Americans aren't about to unanimously agree to give up guns or video games. But no matter how divided we are over gun control or censorship, we should still be able, as decent human beings, to unite in a mighty movement against school violence. It is to our everlasting shame that we haven't.

The country must reassess its educational priorities—and soon. What poses a more immediate danger to the future of public education, standardized tests or gun violence, school vouchers or homemade pipe bombs? The spilled blood of students calls out in answer.

I live in fear that the violence that occurred in Santee—and in Littleton, Colorado, and Conyers, Georgia, and Pearl, Mississippi, and Paducah, Kentucky—will someday occur in Highland, the friendly little community in upstate New York where I serve on the school board. I often wonder how board members in communities bloodied by school shootings must feel. Are they haunted by sorrow and guilt? Do they ask themselves what they might have done differently? I try to push such awful questions out of my mind but can't. Maybe none of us should, as long as children go to school under the shadow of the gun.

4

CENSORSH*T

As a longtime school board member, I should have been accustomed to inopportune phone calls from disgruntled taxpayers and parents, but nothing had prepared me for the call I got that August night. I was just about to sit down to watch a well-deserved video with my family when the phone rang. It was a father calling to complain about the book his fifteen-year-old daughter had been assigned to read over the summer— Maya Angelou's autobiography, *I Know Why the Caged Bird Sings*. I would later find out that the book, which recounts the sufferings of a black girl growing up in the Depression-era South, is one of the books most frequently banned from schools, along with R. L. Stine's Goosebumps series and J. D. Salinger's *Catcher in the Rye*.

Now, a week before school started, the father wanted to know who had chosen the book as required reading for all students entering 10th grade. The high school English teachers, I told him. He called them "incompetent," and their choice "irresponsible." I reminded him that Angelou had read a poem at Bill Clinton's presidential inauguration. For someone like me, who has childhood memories of craggy, white-haired Robert Frost, the grand old man of American letters, reading "The Gift Outright" at John F. Kennedy's inauguration in 1960, this confirmed her literary pedigree. I hadn't quite realized yet that the father was critiquing morals, not literature.

He asked if I had ever read *I Know Why the Caged Bird Sings.* I admitted, with a twinge of embarrassment, that I hadn't. Egotism tempted me to add that I was nonetheless familiar with the poem by Paul Laurence Dunbar from which the title was drawn—"I know why the caged bird sings, ah me/When his wing is bruised and his bosom sore"—but somehow I resisted. I just mentioned that my oldest daughter, also fifteen and a prospective sophomore, had read the book during the summer and liked it.

The father urged me to examine for myself chapters 11, 12, and 35, claiming that they contained graphic sex. I assured him that I would and then, in an attempt to end our conversation on a helpful note, recommended that he speak to the principal about having his daughter read another book in place of Angelou's. "You're missing the point," he said. The point was that the book was inappropriate not just for his kid, but for all the kids in 10th grade, and should be banned. For the first time, I understood exactly what I was facing. A bubble of fear welled up inside me.

Even before alerting the superintendent to this disturbing call, I retrieved the book from my daughter's room and sat down at the kitchen table to read the offending chapters. In chapters 11 and 12, Angelou recalls being sexually abused as a child by her mother's live-in boyfriend, while in chapter 35 she describes sexually blundering about as a confused adolescent. There is nothing the least bit sexy about the sex that occurs in the book. It is presented in terms of violence and victimization. Rather than lewd or offensive, I found the chapters heartbreaking.

But would others? Or could I expect more calls from outraged parents? And what about my fellow board members? How would they react to repeated demands for censorship? They weren't aware, as I was from years of writing and teaching journalism, of the long, heroic struggle for freedom of thought and expression that began with poet-pamphleteer John Milton during the Puritan Revolution in England. "Give me the liberty to know, to utter, and to argue freely according to conscience, above all liberties," Milton wrote. Would the board agree? Would the community?

I was right to wonder. Just a day after the father called me all upset, a mother called to protest as well. She gave a one-word review of Angelou's book: "Disgusting!" I might have told her that *I Know Why the*

Caged Bird Sings was nominated for the National Book Award in 1970 and that the State Education Department has since included it on a list of approved readings for high school students. I might also have pointed out that the sexual violence and exploitation described in the book reflect a growing problem; one recent survey found that four of five students in grades 8 through 11 have experienced some sort of sexual harassment in school. Lastly, I might have suggested that a much greater threat than Angelou to children's health and morals is their routine exposure to mass-mediated messages—commercials that use sex to sell clothes and cosmetics, music videos that use sex to sell CDs, movies that use sex and blood to sell tickets.

But I didn't. I listened to the mother without interrupting and then thanked her for her input and hung up. I was saving my arguments for the board, which had a regularly scheduled meeting that very night.

It turned out that all the board members had been contacted by the disgruntled parents. Although only one member (call him Joe) openly sided with them, at least two others seemed to be leaning that way. Joe kept asking why the school would assign such a controversial book when thousands of uncontroversial books were available. There was a reasonable answer to this, but the person who had it, the director of curriculum and instruction, was away on vacation. She later told me that *I Know Why the Cage Bird Sings* had been chosen in part because some parents had criticized the previous summer's reading list for not including any books by women or minority authors. Ironically, the attempt to solve one problem had created another.

The points I might have earlier made to the mother I now made to the board. Then, worried I still hadn't gotten through, I added a couple more. I argued that if we banned controversial books from the high school, our students would be unprepared not only for the intellectual challenges of college, but also for the difficult decisions of life. And I noted that the protagonist in a coming-of-age story like *I Know Why the Caged Bird Sings* could provide needed companionship to teenagers, who frequently feel lost and alone in a cold, flat adult world.

The last point was the most important to me, but the hardest for the rest of the board to grasp. That may be because they don't read a lot; in fact, Joe has cheerfully admitted on several occasions that he has trouble understanding the little he does read. He wears his ignorance like a ribbon of merit. Having never recognized his own life struggles in the life struggles portrayed in books, he can't appreciate how anyone else could or would even want to—can't appreciate the power of stories to heal, guide, comfort, instruct. All he can see when he looks at a book that explores what it means to be a man, or a woman, or just human are strange and forbidding words.

Our meeting ended late, but to my relief, without the board banning *I Know Why the Caged Bird Sings*. Instead, we directed the superintendent to reexamine the process for choosing books for the summer reading program. We also agreed that the school would allow a substitute book for students whose families complained. Yet a feeling of crisis lingered, even deepened, over the next few days. The original complainants phoned other parents, urging them to storm a literature circle scheduled for 10th graders. Tipped off to the plan by town gossip, the principal intercepted the raiding party in the hall and marched them down to his office. Students, under the guidance of an English teacher, were able to discuss *I Know Why the Caged Bird Sings* unmolested— for now.

Curriculum experts have proposed a number of measures to prevent battles over censorship from breaking out. They say parents should be invited to contribute to the development of school reading programs. They say teachers should maintain files of professional reviews that support reading selections. They say schools should give recommended, rather than required, reading lists. These are all good ideas and worth trying. But having recently lived through a censorship scare, I'm less confident than ever about the efficacy of either rules or reason. We have people among us, some of them right on our school boards, who fear books and distrust education, and once they get fired up there is just no telling how far the flames will spread.

5

SCHOOL BOARD BLUES

School board members are chosen by sacred democratic process to do an impossible job with inadequate resources. This, in my experience, is the first principle of school board membership. The second principle is even worse to contemplate: school board members are held responsible for everything, but have control over nothing. If you don't recognize these two principles, my guess is that you haven't been a school board member very long.

I can illustrate the first principle by reference to what has now become a familiar scenario. Your state education department, after decades of expecting the minimum from students, finally decides to raise academic standards. But does the state offer a legible map of how to get students from here to there? No. Does it increase aid to your district enough to help pay for the journey? No. Do teachers temper their salary demands during contract negotiations so you will have some money left to buy new textbooks? No. Do local taxpayers agree in a spirit of cooperation and community to shoulder the costs of improvement? No again. It is usually at this point that school board members begin to doubt not only the value, but also the sanity of school board membership.

My quarrel isn't with higher standards. Our future as a free society depends largely on the quality of the education citizen-students receive.

Rather, my quarrel is with the fact that state education departments mandate lofty goals, then give school boards the least possible resources to achieve them. You might just as well ask a construction gang to excavate for a foundation using only spoons—plastic ones.

But who gets blamed by parents and the press when impossible goals aren't met? Why, the school board! It sometimes seems that the role of the board isn't to lead educationally, but to take punches for other institutions in society, from the postmodern family to big government.

Of course, nobody on a school board absorbs more punishment than its president, who supposedly occupies a position of honor and prestige but actually serves as a convenient target for public criticism. After a while, the board president comes to feel like one of those life-size models of deer that bow-hunters use for practice—defenseless and full of holes. Classes taking too many, or not enough, field trips? Either way, it is your fault. Football team having a losing season? Also your fault. Teacher out with an inoperable brain tumor? Yep, your fault.

What vocal critics of school boards seem to forget is that the boards are made up of unpaid volunteers. Sure, some members nurture larger political ambitions, but most had to be coaxed into running for office by friends and neighbors. Their reward for extending themselves is several years of being second-guessed, berated, and even demonized. It is one thing not to receive any pay for board work; it is quite another to never receive a kind word.

Under these conditions, who in his or her right mind would want to be a school board member? The answer is: practically nobody. Fanatics and chronic malcontents will always be available to seek election, but credible candidates have grown scarce in most communities. Moreover, experienced board members are increasingly difficult to retain. Just when their experience should be ripening into wisdom, they resign in frustration or hunker down and serve out the remainder of their terms grudgingly and without hope. Which leads me to a third principle of school board membership: idealism and enthusiasm tend to diminish in direct ratio to a person's number of years on the board.

Not a few veteran board members of my acquaintance have concluded that the whole school board system has outlived its usefulness. And they may be right. Local control of schools exists more or less in name only today. Boards no longer define what the urgent issues in their districts are but have these defined for them by the state and federal governments, the media, educational consultants, unions, and so on. With the world seeming to spin faster and faster all the time, and social complexities expanding centrifugally, boards exercise about as much influence on the actual outcome of events as would human sacrifice, another once-popular institution.

But perhaps we shouldn't write off school boards as utterly futile just yet. If boards, despite interminable meetings and sincere effort, can't do obvious good, they can still prevent others from doing obvious harm. This is no small responsibility. Ethicists even have a term for it. They call it the "duty of nonmaleficence."

Of the various factions at large in a school district (teachers, administrators, students, taxpayers, board), only the board is so situated or motivated as to be able to see each interest in relation to every other. Teachers identify the right and the true for the most part with what will benefit teachers; administrators, with what will benefit administrators; taxpayers, with what will benefit taxpayers. It is the board's duty to try to keep this sort of instinctive self-seeking within bounds. Think public education is a mess now? Just imagine the mess if schools were operated primarily for the benefit of mediocre teachers or miserly taxpayers rather than for the benefit of students. Oops! That is how many are operated.

All of us who serve on school boards sometimes lose heart. Our work is mocked or peevishly questioned, when it isn't just ignored. But like Beckett's tramps, we must go on despite fatigue and cold and disappointment. For if we didn't carry the ideals of public education the next few steps, tell me, who would?

6

PUBLIC SPEAKING, PRIVATE NIGHTMARE

Most school board members would talk and talk and talk at board meetings if time permitted, and some do it even though time doesn't. But take the same talkative board members and invite them up to the podium to make a speech, and suddenly their desire to spout off disappears. Just the thought of making a speech is enough to turn many of them into nervous wrecks. They don't see themselves charming the audience with their eloquence and wit. Rather, they see themselves stammering and sweating as the audience grows bored, then impatient, and finally hostile.

And they aren't the only ones afflicted with such nightmares. According to *The Book of Lists,* the No. 1 fear among Americans is speaking before a group. It is greater than their fear of dogs, loneliness, flying, death, sickness, deep water, financial problems, insects, and heights. I have never been quite able to understand how people can be more afraid of speaking before a group than dying, but maybe there is an advantage to death that I'm overlooking.

As part of their responsibilities, school board members are sometimes required to make speeches. Board officers in particular are expected to say at least a few words at honor society inductions, ribbon cuttings and groundbreakings, retirement dinners, and, of course, graduations. What can they do to prevent these occasions from becoming embarrassments for them, and cruel and unusual punishment for their audiences? Franklin Delano Roosevelt had a couple of ideas.

Asked his advice on public speaking, FDR, one of the great speakers of modern times, recommended, "Be brief and be seated." While sitting down when you are done isn't a bad idea, being brief is probably more important. There is as little to be gained in being long-winded in a speech as there is in being slow-footed in a race. An audience will listen politely to almost anything you have to say if you keep it short, but go on and on and you risk public-speaking disaster. The audience will begin to feel like they are stuck in a kind of verbal traffic jam, with no exit in sight and exhaust fumes poisoning their brains.

Although you may be flattered (as well as somewhat panicked) to be invited in your capacity as a board member to make a speech, you should try to remember that you are rarely, if ever, the star attraction. People don't come to high school graduations to hear you or me speak; they come to see their children receive—at last!—their diplomas. This doesn't mean you shouldn't prepare your speech with care. It just means that your speech is usually an accompaniment to the main meal, an appetizer or an aperitif, not the meal itself. Whatever you have to say should enhance people's appetite for the meal or aid their digestion after.

But what do you have to say? Unfortunately, if you are like a lot of board members, not too much. The typical speech by a board member is a random series of educational cliché ("Every child can learn," "It takes a village," "The future belongs to the well-educated"), introduced by an unfunny joke and interspersed with thank-yous, inspirational quotes, and questionable statistics, all tied together by mere proximity. To top it off, the speaker is often terrified, as though having just seen the decomposed corpse of his or her grandmother in the audience, and delivers the speech with a dry mouth and a small, squeaky, stricken voice.

Which is a shame, because board members don't get that many opportunities to address five hundred, or even fifty, people at once. Almost no one shows up at the twice-monthly meetings of the board on which I serve except those of us who have to be there. About the only time we ever draw a crowd is when the public is mad at us, in which case the smell of blood is in the air, and we might as well be the mute, misunderstood monster in *Frankenstein* that is pursued through the night by angry peasants armed with pitchforks and clubs. For a board member to have a large and generally receptive audience, as happens at graduations and awards banquets, is a rare privilege. Don't squander it by sounding like a victim of lockjaw or by saying things you have already heard others say.

A speech must be personally significant to the speaker before it can be personally significant to anyone else. The best speeches come from the heart as much as from the head. Chief Joseph of the Nez Percé provides a powerful historical example. When he and his people were ordered to move from their lands in the Oregon Territory to a reservation in Idaho, they tried to flee to Canada, traveling over fifteen hundred miles and fighting several battles along the way with the U.S. Army. When they finally surrendered on October 5, 1877, Chief Joseph poured out his despair:

> Tell General Howard I know his heart. What he told me before, I have it in my heart. I am tired of fighting. Our Chiefs are killed; Looking Glass is dead, Ta Hool Shute is dead. The old men are all dead. It is the young men who say yes or no. He who led the young men is dead. It is cold, and we have no blankets; the little children are freezing to death. My people, some of them, have run away to the hills, and have no blankets, no food. No one knows where they are—perhaps freezing to death. I want to have time to look for my children, and see how many of them I can find. Maybe I shall find them among the dead. Hear me, my Chiefs! I am tired; my heart is sick and sad. From where the sun now stands I will fight no more forever.

Chief Joseph was known to his people as "Thunder Traveling to the Loftier Mountain Heights." His speech, encapsulating in its candid details and spare, poetic phrasing the destruction of the American Indian, suggests the name was more than justified.

Audiences don't necessarily have to hear thunder when you or I speak. But they should be able to hear at least some of the noise of life's battles. All of us maintain a stock of stories—stories about growing up, going to school, choosing a career, raising children. Somewhere among these stories are themes for speeches, or if not exactly themes then the concrete examples that give themes their definition and drama. Emerson once said every man's life could be a book. Well, guess what? It could also be a speech.

Thus far, we have discussed the need for a public speaker to be brief, to avoid clichés, to speak in an authentic voice, and to tell stories that compel attention. That is a lot, but still not all the speaker must do. Additionally, the speaker must decide how to organize the speech, who its target audience is, and whether to deliver the speech from memory or notes.

> *Organization:* Avant-garde director Jean-Luc Goddard, when asked by a journalist whether his films have a beginning, middle, and end, replied, "Yes, they do, but not in that order." Too often audiences get the same feeling about speeches, that they aren't organized to be easily followed. A speech can be organized in many different ways, including chronologically (from first to last) or thematically. The key is to pick an appropriate pattern and then stick to it throughout. Otherwise, the speech will be just a pile of parts, like a disassembled machine for which the instructions for assembly have been lost.

> *Target Audience:* Sometimes you face an audience of all teachers, or all students, or all parents. Other times, and these are worse, you face a mixed audience of teachers *and* students *and* parents *and* grandparents *and.* . . . When that happens, which group should be your target audience? Speaking once at a middle school graduation, I aimed my speech directly at the graduates, who, being young and agile, ducked. I learned from that experience that you can never have too many targets. Aim at everyone in the audience and you are bound to hit someone.

> *Delivery:* Whether you speak from notes or extemporaneously, you should breathe normally, make eye contact with the audience, and use a conversational tone of voice. Paradoxically, it takes practice to appear natural and relaxed. I practice a speech half a dozen times or more, working particularly on my intonation and gestures, before I actually deliver it. My children find this amusing, while the family dog seems merely mystified.

It is too bad that being a loud-mouth isn't the primary qualification for being a public speaker. If it were, some school board members would be not just good public speakers but great ones. Public speaking requires preparation, intelligence, and calm courage, which, come to think of it, are qualities that should be required for board membership as well.

7

INTO THE FIRE

One evening as I waited for my son, a fullback on the varsity soccer team, to limp across the field after a hard-fought game, a woman came up to me.

"You're president of the school board, right?"

She looked normal enough, so I agreed I was.

"Well," she said, "a stair's loose over there." She jerked her head in the general direction of the bleachers.

I think she expected me to go to the trunk of my car, take out a toolbox, and repair the stair myself. Regardless, she appeared disappointed when I just thanked her and told her I would pass on the information.

This is a fairly typical incident. Not many people seem to understand a board president's role. Most apparently believe it is to listen to their stupid suggestions and petty complaints. Just the other day, a man cornered me at another soccer game and went into a long, complicated disquisition on the advantages of paving a small patch of district property rather than seeding it. I kept examining his face for some sign that he was putting me on. But, no, he was absurdly in earnest.

A lot, too much perhaps, has been written about the qualities a leader needs. Hundreds of books and magazine articles promise to reveal the twenty-one laws, or the four steps, or the seven secrets of effective leadership. I have even discovered a website that draws leadership lessons from the bloody triumphs of twelfth-century Mongol ruler Genghis Khan. But the public doesn't want a khan as board president, a warrior-king whose fierce eyes glitter with visions of world conquest. The public wants someone who can answer why there is no liquid soap in the dispensers in the elementary school bathrooms.

The most intriguing comment about leadership I have ever read is also the most ominous. It comes from *Pirke Abot,* or *Ethics of the Fathers,* a two-thousand-year-old collection of Jewish maxims and sayings. One saying, attributed to Rabbi Johanan, warns, "Woe to leadership, for it buries those who possess it." Since assuming leadership of the board a couple of years ago, I have often pondered this saying, feeling for its bottom as anxiously as a weak swimmer feels with the tips of his or her toes for the bottom of a pool.

Why "Woe to leadership"? Is it because leaders toss and turn all night, haunted by their responsibilities and dark dreams of failure? Or is it because even a small dose of power can act like a hallucinogen, corrupting their judgment, deranging their sense of proportion? Or perhaps it is because leaders are always under suspicion, targets of criticism and gossip. I myself am rumored of have arranged, in the suave manner of a modern Mafia don, special privileges at school for my kids and the kids of my friends. I guess some people just can't conceive that others might be willing to serve the public interest rather than their own.

When I was campaigning for my first term on the school board, I shook hands on the street with a man who half-jokingly said, "You must like aggravation." I laughed, thinking I knew exactly what he meant. I thought he meant board members must deal with disgruntled parents and whiny taxpayers and incompetent teachers. But it wasn't until I had to try to lead the board that I learned what real aggravation is.

Board members tend to treat the board president, whom they elect from their own opinionated ranks, with a kind of ironic deference. They will give the president a gavel and a seat at the head of the table, but won't necessarily heed the president's advice or gaveling during meetings. There have been times when I have stared at the gavel in my hand and wondered what possible use the thing can have. All I have been able to figure out so far is this: if you can't bear anymore to hear board members scream at the superintendent or fight with each other, you can aim the gavel at the middle of your forehead and—thwack!—knock yourself out.

A board president has the unenviable task of having to somehow unite a bunch of loud, recalcitrant board members without actually supergluing them together. The solution, I think, begins with distinguishing between leading and controlling. Controlling is intimidating or manipulating people into doing what you want them to do. Leading is inspiring them to do what they should want to do in the first place. For school boards, this is always doing what is educationally best.

My predecessor as board president was the bullying type. At meetings she would huffily gather her things and begin packing up to go home if any of us dared to challenge her judgment. Once or twice she even threatened to resign. I wish now that we had let her, but for reasons no longer clear to me, nervousness or perhaps simple inertia, we didn't, and she wound up presiding over the board for three straight years, honking and hissing throughout like an angry goose. By the time I became president, morale in the district was alarmingly low. Four of our six top administrators had just fled to other jobs, and the superintendent, when not crying in her office, was contemplating joining the outrush. As for the board, they had the pale, hollow-eyed appearance of victims of some mysterious intestinal misery.

The situation called for action, but what kind? I once saw on TV the leader of a grimy crew of smokejumpers explain how he and his men, all Blackfeet Indians, approach their dangerous work. He talked about "respecting the fire," its speed and cunning and power. "We try to do what we can," he said, "and no more than we have to." This seems like a sound philosophy, whether you are fighting a monster forest fire out West or guiding a school board through the murk of human decision making.

I have tried in the role of board president to do what I can and no more than I have to. I have tried to stay within my sphere of authority and leave the day-to-day running of the district to the principals and superintendent. I have tried to lead by quiet example and not bully board members into agreement. I have tried to listen respectfully to what people have to say, no matter how stupid or annoying. I have tried, but of course, I have largely failed. And that is why the rabbi proclaimed, "Woe to leadership," why I wake up with a start in the middle of the night, why, even after all this time, the forest is still burning.

8

SCHOOL BOARD NOTEBOOK

It's called the Broccoli Factor. As a school board member stands in the produce aisle of the local supermarket, trying to decide which bunch of broccoli to buy, constituents invariably come up to him or her to check out a rumor or complain about a teacher. I once considered this, in my early enthusiasm for public service, democracy at work. I now consider it just another reason to hate food shopping.

When you're on a school board, friends may come and go, but enemies accumulate.

The superintendent was discussing the state aid picture at a board meeting, and it wasn't a Cezanne. For the eighteenth year in a row, the legislature was late in passing a budget. District voters had approved our own budget months ago, but the amount of state aid available to help pay for it had shrunk alarmingly since then. In fact, the superintendent said, the shortfall might be as much as $600,000. The more she talked, the more agitated and depressed the board became. We realized that we might very well be forced to slash instructional programs, or raise taxes, or both. Someone asked what we could do about it. The superintendent said some of us could visit the local office of our state senator. Wearing ski masks, I thought to myself.

I have a big birthday coming up—the big 5-0, though it feels more like the big uh-oh.

The daughter of one of our janitors has been suspended by the middle school principal for five days after beating another girl's head against the wall. Her mother thinks the suspension is somehow unfair and stamps into the superintendent's office to protest. Later the same day, she calls the superintendent on the phone to protest some more. The superintendent is unmoved and refuses to lift or even reduce the suspension. The frustrated mother, before hanging up, snarls what for her must be a *bon mot:* "I guess it's not who you know, it's who you blow."

A school district is almost surreal in the complexity of its operations, like a nightmarish chess game in which the pieces won't stay where they have been moved; the rules are revised without consultation or warning; and the chess board itself, while clearly marked in white and black, keeps floating up from the table and sailing around the room, chased fruitlessly by players who can no longer remember the original point of the game.

A bad week so far, yet no worse than most. Two varsity football players confess (after the athletic director threatens to cancel the rest of the season) to urinating on the helmets and pads of the JV team. The attractive blond director of curriculum and instruction, the board's pet, announces her intention to resign to take a better-paying job in a nearby district, though she has just received a raise here. The high school principal, whose thick layer of blubber has earned him the sardonic nickname "Tiny" among teachers, discovers he has diabetes and turns moody and incommunicative, spending more and more time alone in his office with the door closed. The superintendent, all in a panic, recommends that the board rent a retired superintendent for $400 a day to fill the administrative gaps, and the board, in the grip of either temporary insanity or permanent stupidity, agrees. The local police, extra vigilant since the terrorist attacks of September 11, report a rumor circulating through town that the blueprints for the high school have been stolen as part of a plot to blow up the building. Oh, don't I wish.

A fellow board member: "It takes three years (the length of a term) to do anything; it takes six years to do anything right."

The other day I was stopped at a light behind an older, slightly rusted gray Subaru (the kind of car a graduate student in English might drive) plastered with politically progressive bumper stickers. We Recycle. I Don't Eat Anything With a Face. Honor Native American Treaties. Children Are People. Women Make Great Leaders/You're Following One. As I was smiling to myself at the slogans, a slender hand appeared out the driver-side window and dropped a still-burning cigarette into the street. And I thought for the thousandth time about the human predilection for words and lies and desecrations. Then the light changed.

Imagine a giant, gelatinous blob—a blob the size, say, of a high school gym—towering over you. If you push it here, it bulges out there. If you attempt to climb over it, you sink into it instead. Now imagine that there are human bodies suspended in the blob, like mini-marshmallows in a bowl of Jell-O, and that the bodies belong to students, teachers, administrators, and school board members, and you will begin to understand the grotesque nature of educational bureaucracy, just how controlling and all-encompassing it is and how difficult to reform. True, sometimes the blob moves, but agonizingly and without coordination, one part lurching ahead while other parts drag along or remain stuck in place. When this happens, the bodies inside bend and bounce, giving the appearance of purposeful movement. But it is only an appearance. The blob has no purpose except its own tenacious growth. Imagine something the color of sickness and the weight of medicated sleep spreading slowly, slowly over you.

Being on the school board appeals to my vanity. I like the fact that school bus drivers wave to me when the buses go by my house. I like the fact that when I identify myself on the phone, the school secretary suddenly loses the chill in her voice and becomes warm and deferential. I like the fact that teachers take me aside at school functions and give me the inside scoop on the textbook situation or classroom crowding, adding half-defiantly, half-apologetically, "I just thought you should know." Although I sometimes say otherwise, I even like the fact that people stop me around town to offer ill-informed advice. This kind of attention may be what keeps certain board members coming back for a second and third and fourth term despite the inherent frustrations of the job. If that is indeed the case, maybe vanity isn't such a bad thing after all. Then again, considering the records of many long-serving board members, I'm not sure it's actually an essential qualification for public office either.

The later the hour, the worse the decision; or, after midnight, everyone's an idiot.

There was a rattling of tin cups at the last board meeting. One contingent of moms begged us to hire more aides for their children's kindergarten classes, while an even larger contingent begged us to fund a JV cheerleading squad for their thirteen- and fourteen-year-old daughters. Then a contingent of teachers begged us to buy new social studies textbooks (some of those in use at the middle school have a copyright date of—ready for this?—1979). The board listened with apparent sympathy, but I knew that, like me, the other members were trying to harden themselves against the various pleas, the way you might harden yourself against a panhandler sprawled pathetically across your path. At the local level, where the resources are often few and the needs often numerous, the art of governing resides not so much in balancing competing interests as in somehow ignoring them.

Anytime there is an unequal distribution of power, as there is between teacher and students in a classroom, injustice is not only possible, it is perhaps inevitable.

A first-grade teacher, a tall, bony woman in her early thirties with a cadaverous face and an irritatingly assured voice, overheard explaining her teaching philosophy: "I'm not the 'huggy' type of teacher. I'd rather have students respect me than hug me. Besides, they always have runny noses and I don't want to catch their colds."

Here I am entering my fifties, the so-called "Dangerous Decade" because the risk of death from heart disease, stroke, and cancer goes way up. Why should I spend another precious minute serving on a school board, especially when the public is so prone to criticize and second-guess us? Why not do something more fun, like kayak the upper reaches of the Hudson, as I have long wanted to do? My son Graham, a senior in high school, recently asked himself a similar question. After reading in the paper that the September 11 terrorists may have nuclear weapons, he wondered why he should bother to finish an essay on *Othello* he was writing for AP English. He ruefully shook his head as he told me this. Although I probably could have said something to pick him up, I just ruefully shook my head, too. There *is* a certain absurdity in finishing your homework when, at any moment, you might find yourself wandering with your skin burned off through a radioactive wasteland. And yet Graham did eventually finish his. What other choice was there? His teacher wasn't very likely to accept existential nausea as an excuse, was she?

I have heard of school boards that make the Donner Party sound well organized—boards that argue for argument's sake, that distrust all administrators, or that bog down in meaningless details. My own board doesn't have these kinds of problems, though the loss of even one current member in the spring election could conceivably tip things over. As elected officials, board members should be responsive, I suppose, to the will of the people. But what if the will of the people is misguided? What if the people prefer low taxes to high student achievement, or jerks to genuine leaders? What then? Board members have an important job to do; they just often do it badly. A number of states, in an attempt to improve the performance of school boards, have begun requiring annual training for board members. Some consider this an assault on local autonomy, but better that than to be stranded among the rocks and snow with nothing to eat except each other.

My wife bought me a kayak for my birthday. It is still in its original mummy-like wrapping, but I can picture it, low-slung and sleek, a raspberry red, underneath all the plastic and cardboard. I won't remove the wrapping until mid-April, when the last of the ice is finally gone. Meanwhile, I read about day-tripping on the Old Erie Canal and study pullout maps of Adirondack lakes and ponds, with their amoebic shapes and

American Indian names. There are no budget shortfalls up there, no complaining parents, no personnel issues. Silver ghosts of morning mist float eerily across the water, and a kingfisher stands motionless on a half-submerged log as if posing for its portrait. In my mind, I paddle and drift, paddle and drift, and never grow tired and never get lost and never reach the end of exploring.

9

SCHOOL PICTURES

In the 1999 movie *Music of the Heart,* Roberta Guaspari, a super-motivated teacher played by Meryl Streep, overcomes hostile colleagues, skeptical parents, and grim sociological conditions to establish a successful violin program for inner-city kids. Then one morning she arrives at school and discovers that she has been fired. "The board of education cut the budget," her principal (Angela Bassett) explains. "The district had to comply. As of the end of this term, the violin program has been excessed." When Roberta protests that her program is thriving, with 150 children involved and many more clamoring to get in, the principal can only reiterate, "They slashed the budget. . . . As far as the board is concerned, violin classes are *not* a priority." Or, as one of Roberta's young students poignantly puts it, "They don't want music anymore."

If the negative portrayal of the board of education in *Music of the Heart* were just an isolated incident, it would be of little interest or significance. But I have found more than a half-dozen movies dating back to the mid-1950s that portray boards as futile at best and vicious at worst, an unattractive collection of figureheads, old farts, and control freaks. While this negative on-screen image may not be the most pressing issue facing board members today, it does suggest something disturbing about their status in American culture. Assuming that Hollywood movies offer a kind of index to popular attitudes and values, a common enough assumption among cinema scholars, then the public apparently regards boards of education with a dislike bordering on revulsion.

In *Music of the Heart*, Roberta openly challenges the board's decision, issuing a call to arms to parents at the school's spring concert: "This beautiful concert that you've just heard could be the very last concert of the East Harlem Violin Program." (The audience gasps.) "The board of education and the district superintendent think music isn't important for our kids. But they're wrong, and they're going to get a big fight." (The audience erupts in cheers.) Ultimately, the program is saved, though not because the board restores funding but because great violinists like Isaac Stern and Itzhak Perlman stage a glittering benefit concert for it at Carnegie Hall. Despite the happy outcome, there lingers the afterimage of the board as the Osama bin Laden of education, dangerously out of touch with the community and willing to destroy children's futures for budget reasons.

It is an image that recurs in other movies, including *Carried Away* (1996) and *Sing* (1989). In *Carried Away*, an indie production based on Jim Harrison's novel *Farmer*, the board of education plans to shut a two-room rural schoolhouse at the end of the year. The school's teachers, Joseph Svenden (Dennis Hopper) and Rosealee Hensen (Amy Irving), urge the board at a meeting, held in one of the classrooms and crowded with parents, to keep the school open. Asked by a board member what this tiny school offers that the schools in town don't, Joseph says, "A chance to gain the basics without being bused sixty miles a day after getting up at dawn to do chores." The parents murmur their agreement. Interestingly, while traditional symbols of American democracy are conspicuously on display in the scene (old-fashioned wooden desks, a flag, the honest, homely Norman Rockwell faces of farm folks), it soon becomes obvious that the meeting is an empty ritual and that the three-member board isn't there to receive citizen input, but to confirm a predetermined decision.

> **Joseph:** You've already made your mind up about this. There's nothing I can say here today that's going to make any difference, is there?
> **First Board Member:** No, I'm afraid that's true. We don't see any reason why we should reconsider the matter.

Joseph: Then why the hell did you let me waste my time talking to you?
Second Board Member: We don't need that kind of language, Mr. Svenden.
Joseph: That's because you're a bunch of pompous assholes. (Parents laugh in the background.)
Third Board Member: Mr. Svenden, I believe you owe this board an apology.
Joseph: For what? No rule says I can't call an asshole an asshole.

Board members are excoriated in similar terms in *Sing,* a movie that somewhat crazily combines elements of *Romeo and Juliet, Fame,* and The Godfather series. In one scene, a mother, shaking with rage, tells the board president, "Elliot Frye, you were a pimply-faced, four-eyed schmuck in twelfth grade, and you're still a schmuck and a royal pain in the ass," which isn't exactly the kind of comment likely to further democratic debate or the development of rational public policy. But the board itself is hardly an example of democracy in action. To the contrary, its decision to close Central High, a failing school in a crummy Brooklyn neighborhood, clashes with the community's expressed wishes. Parents and teachers, even students, plead with Frye (Yank Azman) at a packed board meeting to keep Central open, or at least allow the annual musical competition between seniors and underclassmen (the "Sing" of the title) to be held one last time. He refuses. Speaking with exaggerated slowness, as if to small (and extremely stupid) children, he says, "We—don't—have—the—budget."

In both *Sing* and *Music of the Heart,* music introduces hope and beauty into young, prematurely blighted lives and becomes a symbol of community identity and pride. Music also figures largely in the cult classic *Rock 'n' Roll High School* (1979), but symbolizes something very different there—the rebellious spirit of adolescence. The students at Vince Lombardi High blast the songs of the punk band the Ramones over the school's PA system and dance in the halls and classrooms, to the neglect of their lessons and the utter dismay of their elders. "Never before has the school board seen a student body such as this," the board president (Grady Sutton) complains. To regain control over these hormonally deranged teenagers, the board appoints a new principal, the witchy-looking Miss Evelyn Togar (Mary Woronov). Unfortunately, like all too many personnel decisions by boards in real life, this one doesn't work out quite as planned. The Ramones show up at the school in person, triggering a riot that climaxes with the students burning down the building, an ending that presumably contained more laughs before Columbine and other recent explosions of school violence.

Not all school boards in movies are as authoritarian as the board in *Rock 'n' Roll High School*, but no matter what their political or philosophical leanings, all are portrayed as curiously ineffective. In *Field of Dreams* (1989), the baseball fantasy that made famous the line, "If you build it, he will come," angry parents descend on a board meeting in small-town Iowa, demanding that the writings of a '60s radical be banned from the curriculum. "I say smut and filth like this has no place in our schools," a mother tells the board to wild applause from the crowd. Although the board president (Mike Nussbaum) tries his best to restore order and reason ("That book you're waving about is hardly smut," he points out. "It is considered by many critics to be the classic novel about the 1960s."), he is quickly shouted down. Only when Amy Madigan, playing a flower-child-turned-farmer's-wife, rises from her seat and speaks with impassioned simplicity for democratic values is the situation saved. "Who's for Eva Braun here?" she says. "Who wants to burn books? Who wants to spit on the Constitution of the United States of America? Anybody? All right! Now, who's for the Bill of Rights? Who thinks freedom is a pretty darn good thing? Come on, come on, let's see those hands. Who thinks we have to stand up to the kind of censorship they had under Stalin? All right! There you go! America, I love you." Throughout this long speech, the board, whose meeting it supposedly is, remains just off-screen in impotent silence.

So even in the rare movie where board members seem to have right on their side, they are still of little use to democracy or education. That is certainly the case in *Our Miss Brooks* (1956), based on a then-popular CBS television program starring Eve Arden as a high school English teacher. In the movie, the principal, Osgood Conklin (Gale Gordon), describes himself as "a man who advocates adherence to regulations—I go by the book." Mr. Stone (Joseph Kearns), the board president, objects to the "iron-handed, autocratic manner" in which Conklin runs the school. "Inasmuch as I consider your dictatorial behavior tantamount to malfeasance," Stone says, "I've petitioned the board to remove you from this position." Conklin reacts with eye-rolling panic, but there is actually nothing for him to worry about, as he would know if he had ever seen a movie with school board members in it. With the characteristic futility of their kind, the board fails to follow through on the petition to fire him.

It is easy to be offended by such movie portrayals when you are a board member. Isn't it bad enough, I kept thinking as I watched *Our Miss Brooks* and the rest, that board members work long hours on thankless tasks for no money? Do we also have to be demonized on the screen, portrayed as arrogant and insensitive and foolish? And yet the portrayal, for all its negativity, may do some good, if only by not-so-subtly reminding us that our first duty isn't to our budgets or our re-elections, but to children. In the black comedy *Teachers* (1984), Nick Nolte, playing a dedicated teacher at war with a smarmy superintendent and a dysfunctional board, makes just that point. "The damn school wasn't built for us," he growls in the closing scene. "It wasn't built for your unions, your lawyers, all your other institutions. It's built for the kids. They're not here for us. We're here for them. That's what it's about—them." To the extent that the movies help us remember this, they can have a positive effect.

But they can have serious negative effects, too. The movies, for example, foster the awful impression that the American public school system is on the verge of a huge nervous breakdown. Most portray teachers as incompetent, students as delinquent, parents as uncooperative, and administrators as self-serving. And grimly presiding over it all is—who else?—a blind, despised, and bumbling board of education.

Perhaps even worse, the movies suggest that protests against the rotten state of things are largely useless. In *Sing, Carried Away,* and *Music of the Heart,* parents and other local residents agitate to save this school or restore that program, but the petty tyrants on the board ignore their pleas. As a fed-up mother says about Frye, the board president in *Sing,* "He's not listening to us. I don't know why we bother."

The movies have no answer to that. If anything, the movies say, Don't bother. By portraying government, even on the grassroots level, as unresponsive to people's needs, the movies legitimize cynicism and apathy. This may be just the message many Americans want to receive, for it excuses their disengagement from the struggles and problems of public life. Sure, our communities are in decline and our schools in crisis, but what can you and I do about it? Not much, according to the movies, not much at all.

SCHOOL BOARD MOVIES
(in chronological order)

Our Miss Brooks (1956)
Directed by Al Lewis
Screenplay by Al Lewis, Joseph Quillan
Cast: Eve Arden (Constance Brooks); Gail Gordon (Osgood Conklin); Don Porter (Lawrence Nolan); Robert Rockwell (Phillip Boynton); Richard Crenna (Walter Denton); Nick Adams (Gary Nolan); Joseph Kearns (Mr. Stone)
Running Time: 85 mins.
Available on VHS

Rock 'n' Roll High School (1979)
Directed by Allan Arkush
Screenplay by Richard Whitley, Russ Dvonch, Joseph McBride
Cast: P. J. Soles (Riff Randell); Vincent Van Patten (Tom Roberts); Clint Howard (Eaglebauer); Dey Young (Kate Rambeau); Mary Woronov (Miss Evelyn Togar); Paul Bartel (Mr. McGee); Grady Sutton (School Board President); The Ramones
Running Time: 93 mins.
Available on VHS and DVD

Teachers (1984)
Directed by Arthur Hiller
Screenplay by W. R. McKinney
Cast: Nick Nolte (Alex Jurel); JoBeth Williams (Lisa Hammond); Judd Hirsch (Roger Revel); Ralph Macchio (Eddie Pilikian); Allen Garfield (Ray Rosenberg); Lee Grant (Dr. Donna Burke); Richard Mulligan (Herbert Gower)
Running Time: 106 mins.
Available on VHS

Sing (1989)
Directed by Richard J. Baskin
Screenplay by Dean Pitchford
Cast: Lorraine Bracco (Miss Lombardo); Peter Dobson (Dominic); Jessica Steen (Hannah Gottschalk); Louise Lasser (Rosie); George DiCenzo (Mr. Marowitz); Patti LaBelle (Mrs. Devere); Yank Azman (Mr. Frye)
Running Time: 99 mins.
Available on VHS

Field of Dreams (1989)
Directed and written by Phil Alden Robinson
Cast: Kevin Costner (Ray Kinsella); Amy Madigan (Annie Kinsella); James Earl Jones (Terence Mann); Ray Liotta (Shoeless Joe Jackson); Burt Lancaster (Dr. Archibald "Moonlight" Graham)
Running Time: 106 mins.
Available on VHS and DVD

Carried Away (1996)
Directed by Bruno Barreto
Screenplay by Ed Jones
Cast: Dennis Hopper (Joseph Svenden); Amy Irving (Rosealee Hensen); Amy Locane (Catherine Wheeler); Julie Harris (Joseph's Mother); Gary Busey (Major Nathan Wheeler); Hal Holbrook (Dr. Evans); Alissa Alban (School Board President); E. J. Morris (School Board Woman); Joe Stevens (School Board Man)
Running Time: 109 mins.
Available on VHS

Music of the Heart (1999)
Directed by Wes Craven
Screenplay by Pamela Gray
Cast: Meryl Streep (Roberta Guaspari); Cloris Leachman (Assunta Guaspari); Aidan Quinn (Brian Sinclair); Gloria Estefan (Isabel Vasquez); Angela Bassett (Janet Williams)
Running Time: 124 mins.
Available on VHS and DVD

10

FLOWER POWER

I may be all thumbs, as a frustrated shop teacher said years ago, but fortunately for me, one of them is green. During the summer, people driving by our house instinctively slow down to look at the big, bright garden out front. I don't grow anything very exotic, mainly flowers native to the region—coneflowers, black-eyed Susans, hollyhocks, yarrow, and bee balm—whose eye-piercing colors decorate the yard like profuse splatters and spirals of spilled paint.

A garden can reward the care and attention of the gardener with more than colorful blooms. As Charles Dudley Warner pointed out in his 1888 classic, *My Summer in a Garden*, gardening teaches "patience and philosophy and the higher virtues—hope deferred, and expectation blighted." Perhaps I toiled too long in the hot sun, or perhaps I have just been toiling too long on a school board, but this summer I was struck by the parallels between gardening and board work.

For example, there is a certain unavoidable drudgery in both. No matter how happy I am each spring to be planting and watering again, by late summer the mere thought of reeling out a hundred-foot hose to soak the thirsty plants can fill me with infinite weariness. It is the same feeling of fatigue I sometimes get when I receive the weekly board briefing, a loose-leaf binder delivered to my door by courier and crammed with the minutes of forgotten meetings, arcane tables and charts, and thick, jargon-ridden reports. Is there duller reading in all the world? Yet if I didn't go through the material and force myself to reflect on it, I would bungle and blunder at the next board meeting, just as if I didn't water, I would massacre the flowers. You can't take the routine drudgery out of either gardening or board work without also taking out the possibility for vitality and growth.

Not that doing a boring job to the best of your ability is any guarantee of success. Just consider what happened to me this summer. I planned my garden down to the smallest detail and tended it scrupulously and watched in gratitude and awe as leaves unfolded and buds emerged. Then, out of the smoky bowels of hell, came a family—the Manson family—of woodchucks. Woodchucks are cute-looking creatures, but rapacious; imagine fuzzy brown slippers with the appetites of garbage disposals. Overnight, they chewed my purple coneflowers to shreds and wounded many other flowers. Even worse, I was defenseless against further attacks. Research revealed that there are no woodchuck repellents on the market, though predator odors, particularly bobcat urine, may be useful. But how was I to find a bobcat in the suburbs, and if I found one, persuade it to pee in a cup?

Gardeners can no more control everything that happens in their gardens than school board members can control everything that happens in their districts. This is why Warner said in his book that a garden teaches philosophy, specifically, a kind of stoicism. The ancient Greek stoics believed that wisdom resided in recognizing what you can't change and submitting to it without anger or bitterness. Board members often behave the exact opposite. Presented with an unfortunate circumstance (a late state budget, an influx of high-needs students, a break in the bathroom pipes), they fall into bitter argument and complaint. They would be wiser to follow the lead of the gardener who feels the loss of his plants to pests or storms, but doesn't extend the destruction by stamping about in a rage.

No one is suggesting that gardeners or board members be passive. Far from it. To keep a garden healthy and productive, a gardener must not only weed regularly, but also prune spent blooms, a practice known as "deadheading," which stops a plant from making seed and allows it to put its energy into making more flowers. There is a moral here for school boards. Rather than continuing to fund programs that have out-lived or failed to prove their usefulness, boards should yank them out by the roots or neatly snip them off. This would free up scarce resources and give surviving programs a better chance to produce results.

The question of productivity hangs like an annoying cloud of gnats over my garden. Every spring my wife lobbies hard for space for veg-etables, and every spring I resist her pleas. Our little war reminds me of the quarrels that occasionally erupt among board members about en-richment programs. Some members are content to offer students only the bare-bones education the state mandates, arguing that music and art classes or Advanced Placement courses are luxuries bound to bankrupt taxpayers. Others answer that music and art contribute to higher test scores in reading and math and that AP courses help kids get into good colleges. While not disputing this, I have my own perspective. It is that in a world increasingly obsessed with consumption—with, if you will, vegetables—boards have an obligation to nurture things that lack obvi-ous utility, whose existences are justified not by their social function or economic value, but by their mystery and grace. Music and art classes and even AP courses are a bit like my flowers: they make the world more beautiful and inhabitable just because they are.

Sadly, beauty can't last. Cold begins to blow down from Canada around Halloween, and soon my garden is a ruin of broken stalks and rusty leaves. The garden exists for long, gray months only as a memory or a future possibility. It takes conscious effort to conjure up the sun-dazzled flowers that once bloomed there or to believe that they will bloom again, orbited by bees and monarchs and swallowtails. Board work requires, I think, a similar optimism—the imagination to see be-yond current problems to better times. None of us who kneel in gardens or sit on school boards can ever know for sure that what we plant will grow. All we can do is drop a seed into the darkness and hope.

II

HONEY AND ASHES

⓫

MOM'S THE WORD

I'm always secretly amused by educators, policymakers, and parents who complain in angry, aggrieved tones about the high-stakes testing now sweeping American public schools. It isn't that I don't share some of their concerns; I do. Like them, I don't want to see teachers primarily "teaching to the test" or students wilting from test anxiety. It's just that I believe pressure is an unavoidable part of academic achievement. And I believe this for good reason—Lillie Good, to be exact.

Lillie Good is my mom. She lives with my dad in a retirement village in Florida, where she divides her time between hustling blue-haired old widows at mah-jongg and visiting doctors of every specialty under the tropical sun. But back when my three brothers and I were growing up in the cold suburban wastes of Long Island, she was an educational leader, at least around our house. She exercised her leadership in a manner that, though certainly effective, would be considered controversial (or perhaps even illegal!) today.

Take the episode of the flash cards. Many parents use flash cards to help their children learn colors, shapes, numbers, and so on. I doubt, however, that any parent has ever used them quite as relentlessly as my mother did when I had trouble memorizing the multiplication tables in third grade. Almost every evening while we kids ate dinner (she generally waited to eat with my dad, who often worked late), she hovered over us, monitoring our intake and flashing at me cards emblazoned with 8 x 6 = and 6 x 7 = and 7 x 9 =. This did little to enhance the flavor of my meatloaf and mashed potatoes or fish sticks and spaghetti, staples of a '50s childhood. Nonetheless, I can now multiply like a whiz, especially with my mouth full.

My mother had sayings that might as well have been on flash cards, so ingrained did they become in my consciousness. One of her favorites was, "Better you cry now than I cry later," which sounds ominous, but wasn't necessarily (unless she was chasing you through the house with a hairbrush when she said it). Most of the time she was just warning my brothers and me that cry and plead as we might, we were destined to live up to her standards rather than she live down to ours.

Unlike today's postmodern parents, who are subjected to a constant media barrage of child-rearing advice from so-called experts, my mom never worried especially about stepping on our rights or damaging our psyches. In fact, I'm not sure she even realized we had psyches. I remember she walked into my room one day and found me drawing at my desk. She wanted to know why I was wasting paper.

Obviously, my mother wasn't a patron of the arts. She saw her job as a parent in strictly pragmatic terms: to prevent us from growing up to be the kind of sons who broke their mother's heart. And what kind of sons was that? The kind who didn't become pre-law or pre-med majors in college.

There was an almost paradoxical, Zen-like quality to some of my mother's sayings, such as "You get out of things what you put into them." She rarely thought I put into them enough. If I got an 80 on a test, she would ask, "Why not 85?" But then if I got an 85 on the next test, she would ask, "Why not 90?" This is still her pattern. Just a few years ago, when I called to tell her that I had been promoted to associate professor, she actually asked, "Why not full professor?"

Although I can laugh now at my mother's tactics, I must admit it is rather rueful laughter. She raised my brothers and me in such a way that we will perhaps never be completely at ease with who we are or what we accomplish. Two brothers are fabulously successful doctors, while the third is a fabulously successful lawyer. Yet I detect in them, as well as in myself, a strange and restless discontent, a hunger that no amount of material wealth or professional recognition seems able to relieve. A great sage once posed the question, "Who is the rich man?" and answered, "He who rejoices in his portion." By that measure, I'm far from rich. Of course, being a teacher, I'm far from rich by any other measure, too.

I suppose the critics of high-stakes testing could point with some justice to my brothers and me as negative examples of what happens to children who are pressured to excel academically. But many students brought up with low academic expectations have worse problems—ignorance, apathy, lack of understanding. Given the demoralizing effects of human stupidity on culture and society, a little carefully applied pressure to educational standards is probably overdue.

The older I get, the more I appreciate the poignancy of my mother's commitment to her sons' education. She was twelve when she went to work, seventeen when she got married, nineteen when she had her first child. If her methods of motivating us sometimes bordered on the brutal, it wasn't because she didn't love us or was incapable of tenderness, but because she believed in her motherly duties with the crazy fanaticism of a kamikaze. She was determined that we do well in school and go to college and become men of science and learning. Now here I am all these years later, a teacher myself, striking tiny golden sparks in the desperate gloom.

Thanks, Mom.

12

HONEY AND ASHES

Growing up, I not only had some teachers who were boring or confusing, but also a few who were truly bad. Bad teachers are bad in the moral sense. They don't necessarily lack an understanding of pedagogy or a knowledge of their subject areas. What they lack more than anything is empathy, the ability to feel with and for others, which philosopher Sissela Bok called "the very foundation of morality."

I was never the type to be the teacher's pet. According to family lore, I couldn't sit still when I was young but was always banging around, which may account for my slovenly appearance in old pictures, my shirt falling out of my pants and my hair sticking up in the back like an effusion of wild ideas. I suppose that if I were a schoolchild today, I would receive calming doses of Ritalin. But in those far-off, more pharmaceutically naïve days, I received instead the contempt of certain teachers.

Three stand out in my mind with peculiar vividness, as if backlit by the flames of hell: Mr. Pitti, Mr. Eakely, and Mr. Gimpel. Mr. Pitti, my 6th grade teacher, was barely taller than his eleven- and twelve-year-old students. He compensated for his small stature by being the biggest bully in the class. One afternoon I was slogging through workbook pages like everyone else when he called me up to his desk. "This isn't your handwriting," he said, jabbing a finger at the homework I had handed in earlier that day.

"It is too my handwriting!" I protested under my breath, trying to keep my voice down so as not to draw attention to us. I had realized in a lurid flash just what Mr. Pitti was suggesting—that someone neater and smarter than my shabby self had done my homework for me.

"No," he insisted, "this isn't your handwriting. I know your handwriting," he paused for dramatic effect, "and this isn't it."

"But I used this pen!" I had carried a blue Bic pen up with me and now waved it in Mr. Pitti's face. "I'll show you."

I pulled my homework toward me and wrote my name in the margin. "There," I said, stepping back with an air of triumph.

Mr. Pitti picked up the paper, examined it for a moment, then gave a short, ugly laugh.

"They're different," he said. He dropped the paper on his desk for me to see.

He was right. The handwritings did look different. Even the color of the ink looked different. I felt sick.

"Go sit down," he hissed.

I haven't forgiven Mr. Pitti yet for treating me with such scorn. I'm not sure I have even forgiven my old classmates for furtively glancing up from their workbooks to watch. It is the invisible wounds, the wounds to our souls and egos, that take the longest to heal.

These were just the kind of wounds my 8th grade English teacher, Mr. Eakley, was adept at inflicting. That year, English consisted mostly of grammar and usage, subjects I found cold and uncongenial, as I also found Mr. Eakely. He was in his forties, extremely tall and thin, with a head that seemed much too large for his pipe-stem body, practically hydrocephalic, an impression only emphasized by the fact that he wore a scanty rust-colored toupee. Although I wasn't fond of either him or grammar, I did love the poems in our literature book. Often when Mr. Eakely was up at the blackboard diagramming sentences, I was at my desk in the back row reading Alfred Lord Tennyson's "The Charge of the Light Brigade" or Alan Seeger's "Rendezvous With Death," thrilling to the stormy music of their lines and their boyish themes of courage and sacrifice.

Because of my frequent unlicensed excursions into poetry, my grades on grammar tests were pretty awful. Once on a literature test, though, I got the only hundred in the class. Mr. Eakely couldn't stomach this; it violated his sense of me as a hopeless moron. Immediately upon returning our tests, and before I could bask in my accomplishment, he said, "You know, the best English students tend to be the worst at literature and vice versa." He wasn't looking at me when he said it, but the words were meant for me, and they were meant to kill.

Mr. Eakely's cruelty was premeditated. Mr. Gimpel's was offhand but no less hurtful for that. He was the junior high football coach and, unfortunately, my 9th grade science teacher, a muscular former jock with a flattop haircut and a ready smirk. One day he was talking about the stars—red giants, white dwarfs, black holes—when he suddenly interrupted himself. "Better close your mouth, Howard," he said, "before something flies in." Apparently, I had been listening to him with my mouth hanging open. He imitated my stupid, slack-jawed expression, and the class laughed. I began right then to hate science.

There is a tradition in Judaism that the first time a child studies Hebrew, he is given a candy or a taste of honey. That is so he will always associate learning with sweetness. Bad teachers create the very opposite associations. They give learning a burnt, bitter taste that lingers on the tongue.

Remembering Mr. Pitti, Mr. Eakely, and Mr. Gimpel, my mouth is full of ashes. They all shared the belief that I was a low achiever, that I couldn't achieve and wouldn't achieve and that I probably shouldn't even try. Sometimes when the moon is dark and I'm alone with my thoughts, I still struggle with the sense of inferiority they took turns embossing on the inside of my skull. It seems a huge price to pay for having been assigned, nearly forty years ago and through no fault of my own, to their classes.

If I could, I would forget all the bad teachers I had and remember only the good. There were a couple—Mrs. Krevorek, who liked my writing or at least pretended to, and Mr. Thompson, who introduced me to the Beat poets and Verdi's operas. But can the good that good teachers do ever completely cancel out the bad that bad teachers do? I don't know. Some say good can't exist without bad. Maybe it is a bittersweet mixture of honey and ashes that holds this sad old beautiful world together.

13

EPITAPH FOR AN ENGLISH TEACHER

He wasn't the most brilliant or stimulating teacher I ever had, just the most influential. His name was Harry Thompson. He taught me Advanced Placement English in 12th grade at John F. Kennedy High School, a class that, strictly speaking, I wasn't prepared for and shouldn't have been allowed to take. That was more than thirty years ago, but I still remember Mr. Thompson with a kind of awe.

Why? It isn't because he was physically impressive. He was a little pear-shaped man with a prematurely bald head that made him look a lot older than he was, only thirty-seven or thirty-eight at the time if my math is correct. And it isn't because he was a flamboyant showman who entertained us with anecdotes and impersonations as he taught. His classroom style was actually rather drab. No, I remember him for the simple reason that he was sympathetic and encouraging to me when so many other teachers would have been the exact opposite.

I ended up in AP English not because of my grades, which were mediocre at best, but because of my mouth, which was large. The class had previously been confined to outstanding students who had followed an accelerated academic track since junior high. Average students like me were exiled to slower, lower-level English classes. I argued that this was elitist. During the political and social turmoil of the late '60s, the argument must have carried a certain weight. The English department let me in.

And, almost immediately, I imploded. Although I harbored ambitions of one day becoming a professional writer, with my name on book covers and idolatrous readers at my feet, I hadn't yet mastered the basics of writing a critical essay. On the first major assignment, a paper on Arthur Miller's play *Death of a Salesman,* I got an ominous "See me" scrawled in red across the top. While the rest of the class trooped off to fifth period lunch, I stayed behind. Sitting on the corner of his desk, Mr. Thompson dissected my paper with harrowing precision, pointing out lapses in interpretation, documentation, even hyphenation. He suggested that perhaps I hadn't put enough effort into the assignment. The truth was worse. I had worked long and hard on the paper. It wasn't lack of effort but sheer ineptitude that accounted for all the mistakes. As he went on reciting my paper's shortcomings, I began to cry tears of frustration and shame.

I had had some teachers earlier in my school career who would have turned cruelly sarcastic at that moment. I had had others who would have remained indifferent. Not Mr. Thompson. He stopped in midsentence, the expression on his face alternating between surprise and concern. He didn't know me well. He didn't know about my literary ambitions. But he made it his business to find out. He became the first adult, beside my parents, to ever show any real interest in me. Over the next year, I brought him my awful poems, and he lent me good books. He encouraged my writing, nurtured my imagination, and protected my dreams. I was just an average student, but he gave me the confidence to be more.

Mr. Thompson can be an inspiring example to all of us who are responsible in one way or another for educating the young—school board members, administrators, faculty, and staff. The educational community gives regular lip service to the notion that "every child can learn." It is time—in fact long past time—to finally put this notion into practice. Mr. Thompson demonstrated how.

First, be sympathetic to those in your keeping. You may have become accustomed to the sight of youngsters struggling with the rigors of growing up, but this is the first time through for them.

Second, never assume that a student is just average. Every student possesses the ability to excel at something worthwhile, whether drawing, science, or friendship.

Third, grades count, but sincerity of effort counts, too.

Fourth and last, the opportunity to teach is ever present: seize it as often as you can.

Harry Thompson died this past summer of a heart attack. His body lay unclaimed in the hospital for several days. He had never married. He had no children. His only surviving relative was an older brother who was sick himself and couldn't get there right away.

But before you decide that Mr. Thompson suffered a tragic end, there is something else you should know. The week he died, he received as a gift a copy of my newest book. I might never have written it or any of my five previous books if he hadn't gathered me up all those years ago. He made a positive difference in at least one child's life. So can you.

(14)

THE AGE OF IMPATIENCE

It seems to me—granted, I'm a cranky person—that we often look in the wrong places for the right things. Want to raise student achievement? Put computers in the classroom. Want to make schools more accountable? Mandate high-stakes testing. Want to improve teaching? Abolish tenure, or increase teacher salaries, or both. No matter how big the problem, we act as if there were a quick answer for it.

But I wonder, would the great sages of old have been even greater if they could have followed the trends or used the tools of modern education? Would Socrates's dialogues, for example, have been any more effective if he had been able to jazz them up with Power Point slides? Or would Hillel, the most revered teacher in Jewish tradition, have been more conscientious if his students had been required to take annual standards-based tests?

Personally, I don't think so. The stories and legends that have come down to us about the sages emphasize the importance of integrity, patience, and love of learning in being a good teacher. There is nothing in the stories about technology, or testing, or any of the other solutions on which we put so much emphasis today.

The qualities of heart and mind that separate good teachers from bad are illustrated in a rabbinic anecdote about Hillel and the leader of a rival school, Shammai. A non-Jew once approached Shammai and said, "Teach me the entire Torah (in effect, all of Judaism) while I stand on one foot." Shammai, who was notorious for his ill temper, beat the man with a ruler. The man then went to Hillel and made the same request, but received a totally different reception. "What is hateful to you," Hillel replied, "do not do to your fellow man; this is the whole Torah, the rest is commentary; go, complete your study."

Hillel's reply is distinguished by its epigrammatic felicity, its loving concern, its ethical zeal. Where Shammai believed that the Torah shouldn't be taught to just anyone, Hillel maintained that it should be taught to everyone. The bad teacher restricts his or her efforts to a special few. The good teacher is democratic and inclusive and treats all students as deserving of encouragement, even the odd and the impudent.

It is perhaps not surprising that one of the most famous sayings attributed to Hillel is, "The impatient cannot teach." (Some versions add, "and the timid cannot learn.") Unfortunately, we live in an impatient age, as a quick look around—who has patience for more?—shows. We bounce from express checking to speed dialing to instant messaging, and gulp fast food in between. But the faster things go, the more impatient we seem to become. We hate worse than ever to stand in line or wait in traffic. We pound our fists and curse when our computers are even a little slow. And if we are impatient with computers that operate at light speed, how long will we wait for teachers and students to get their academic act together?

Not very, it turns out. On January 8, 2002, President Bush signed into law the No Child Left Behind Act, which one educator sarcastically re-dubbed the Leave No Child Untested Act. The law mandates, among other things, that states administer annual tests in reading and math to every student in grades three through eight. Schools whose scores fail to improve could lose federal aid or be forced to replace their teachers and administrators.

On paper (and the No Child Left Behind Act takes up a lot of paper, 1,184 pages), the law may look good. Its promise to get tough on low-performing schools is emotionally satisfying and politically popular. But even so, I can't shake the feeling that the ancient sages wouldn't approve. To them, education was more about instilling a love of learning than about giving tests or making threats.

Both Socrates and Hillel are portrayed in stories as ever eager to learn. Hillel, who was born in Babylonia about 30 B.C., came to Jerusalem for advanced study. For a long time after his arrival, he peddled fuel, using part of his meager daily earnings for food and other personal needs and the rest to pay for admission to school. According to legend, when one day Hillel didn't sell enough wood to meet the admission fee, he climbed to the roof of the schoolhouse so that he might hear the discussions underway indoors. In his concentration he never noticed that it had begun snowing. He was covered in snow and almost frozen to death before his teachers discovered him and brought him down.

The story is intended as a rebuke to those who would cite poverty or the press of business as an excuse for not furthering their learning. This includes teachers. "Teach in order to learn," Indian yogi Baba Hari Dass said, implying that one of the primary rewards of teaching is keeping up with the emergence of new knowledge and ideas. It is also a primary responsibility. Students will forget sooner or later the specific information they learn for a test, but not the love of learning teachers model for them.

Plato's dialogue *Crito*, about the last days of Socrates, provides a moving account of a teacher modeling what one commentator called "the constituent ideals of the civilized mind." In the dialogue, Socrates is in prison, having been sentenced to death for corrupting the youth of Athens with his teachings. Crito, a friend and former student, visits him just before dawn to beg him to escape, but the old philosopher (he is about seventy) refuses. He explains that if he fled to a neighboring city with the help of his supporters, he would be disrespecting the institutions and laws of Athens. And wouldn't that, he asks, be shameful, for hadn't he always taught that "virtue and justice and institutions and laws" were "the best things among men?" He calmly tells Crito that he will drink poison and die rather than betray his principles. It is the ultimate in lesson plans.

Given the sacrifices of Socrates, Hillel, and other legendary sages, it seems almost silly to complain about such things as one-size-fits-all standards and high-stakes testing. Then again, it is perhaps precisely because the sages showed how important teachers can be that we should resist the current trend to reduce teaching to preparing students for tests or learning to do well on them. When will people realize, damn it, that learning isn't about knowing the answer, but about pondering the question?

⑮

THE FAMILY PLAN

My wife and I have—God bless them—four children, two boys and two girls, ranging in age—heaven help us!—from eleven to twenty. While they may have come out of the same kitchen drawer, so to speak, they are as different from each other as knives from spoons, or can openers from corn holders. Nonetheless, we are bound by blood and duty to love each equally and give each an equal chance at happiness. Our situation isn't unlike that of a teacher confronting a classroom filled with students of varying abilities and interests. The teacher is expected to teach them all, the underachiever as well as the overachiever, the dim as well as the bright.

But how? My wife, a wise woman with an ironic sense of humor, believes that the key to raising children, especially teenagers, is to figure out what it is they want to do and then, if it is legal and under your credit-card limit, advise them to do it. She claims this greatly reduces the risk of parental stroke.

And she may be right. Certainly when we tried to bend our oldest to our will, the results were less than impressive. He still got speeding tickets, still failed courses, still hung out with kids who looked like extras from a *Mad Max* movie. We finally realized we couldn't order him to grow up—or, rather, we could, but only at the cost of further eroding our already crumbling relationship with him. Yes, we are disappointed that he flunked out of one college and dropped out of another; yes, we are frustrated that he simply shrugs whenever we ask about his long-term plans. But we are also increasingly aware that life unfolds without much regard for parents' dreams and wishes. He will grow up, just on his own timetable, not ours.

If there is a lesson here for educators, it is perhaps that you can't force children to become what they aren't ready to be. The current nation-wide trend toward more frequent standardized testing seems to ignore this basic fact. Its supporters envision education as a kind of automated assembly line, all students in the same grade learning the same things in the same way with the same outcome. They take little account of the child who develops along a different path or at different pace.

To go back to my oldest, I have often felt that he was at a disadvantage throughout his years of public school because his best qualities weren't among those generally measured by tests or prized by teachers. He has, for example, an uncanny ability to relate to animals, big or small, wild or domestic, fur-bearing or scaly. I have seen him rescue panic-stricken birds that found themselves trapped in our screened-in porch, calming their frightened flapping with his own lack of fear and then scooping them up in his bare hands and setting them free. The birds recognize what standardized tests can't, his gentleness and sympathy. A district may have high test scores, but how good is a school system that treats as insignificant the very qualities a cruel and bloody world most needs?

My second son, unlike the first, is an outstanding student by all the conventional measures—test scores, grade point average, class rank. I would have to add together my grades in two high school courses to equal his grade in one. The real irony, though, is that his school career began rather inauspiciously. Following kindergarten screening, he was assigned to a class for at-risk students. When my wife and I questioned the placement (and who knew him better than we did?), the principal said he could go into a regular kindergarten class, but that if he struggled, it would be our fault. Intimidated by the prospect, we backed down.

That this story has a happy ending, with my son eventually casting off the inaccurate label slapped on him, doesn't mean it is a happy story. To me, it illustrates the difficulty too many parents have in making them-

selves heard above the groaning of a constipated educational bureaucracy. These are challenging times in which to raise children, and parents should at least be able to count on schools as their allies.

I never feel more like I need an ally than when I look at my older
daughter, soon to be fifteen, parading around with her belly button fash-
ionably exposed. Sometimes it seems the whole culture is conspiring to
turn her into a mall-going, instant messaging ding-dong who derives her
role models from MTV, her insights from movies, and her greatest grat-
ification from shopping. And where can a parent get help in beating
back this sea of cultural crud? Not necessarily from schools. The ideology of relentless, ever-escalating consumption—what novelist Ted Rall
bluntly called Americans' obsession with "earning as much as they can
so they can buy as much worthless crap as they can as quickly as they
can"—has penetrated even there. School leaders now often promote education to a skeptical public by emphasizing its role not in preserving
democracy or building character, but in increasing the purchasing
power of graduates.

Isn't it more important to be a good citizen than a smart shopper?
Shouldn't schools be a haven from, and not simply an extension of, the
prevailing commercial culture, with its over-the-top worship of material
success? When so much of society has become infected with the virus of
greed, don't teachers, entrusted with the mental and moral development of the community's children, have an obligation to carry forward
the true values of life?

For the sake of my youngest child, I hope so. She is just entering middle school, which, to the overactive imaginations of anxious parents,
seems like the dark woods in a Grimm's fairy tale, inhabited by evil spir-
its, hairy beasts, and ready-to-bake witches. Research shows that the
American middle school is, in fact, a perennial trouble spot—the
Mideast of public education. Rather than Arabs and Israelis, the casual-
ties are self-worth and academic achievement.

There are people who believe the solution lies in the business world.
They want schools to be product-oriented. They say public education
should adopt the techniques of private industry. In my more cynical mo-
ments, I wonder if this means that school executives should be over-
compensated, school districts merged, and school lunches assembled in
Sri Lanka.

I have another solution. It is that school boards, administrators, faculty, staff, and students acknowledge that our fates are inextricably intertwined and treat each other accordingly, as members of one big raucous family. Of course, we would still have problems and conflicts. What family doesn't? But we would also have the encouragement of knowing that we are, at bottom, more alike than different; that we are bound to each other by golden cords of memory and tradition; that indoors or out, we are surrounded by people who would lift us if we fell and cheer us if we succeeded and love us whatever.

16

THE CONTEMPT SYNDROME

Back in the late 1970s, when I was a novice copyeditor on a daily newspaper in Ann Arbor, Michigan, I first encountered what I have since come to think of as "the contempt syndrome." This syndrome afflicts not just print journalists, however. It gets its name from the tendency of many different kinds of professionals to harbor contempt for the very people they purport to serve. Thus journalists tend to look down on their readers; politicians on their constituents; lawyers, their clients; doctors, their patients; and flight attendants, their passengers. Even teachers look down on their students.

No sane person starts out in a profession secretly despising those he or she is supposed to help. Rather, as the old saying goes, familiarity breeds contempt. It took about six months on the copy desk for me to become familiar enough with newspaper readers to begin despising them for their morbid curiosity and lack of seriousness. I mean, if the readers of the *Ann Arbor News* were serious, would they have wanted so many stories about sex, crime, and the cabbage diet? Would they have voted for their favorite comic strip, but not for president?

Everything about daily journalism (except the salary scale) is fast-paced, and disillusionment with one's clientele may take longer than six months to develop in other, less hectic professions. But whatever the timetable, some degree of disillusionment does eventually set in. Now that I'm a journalism teacher I often feel toward my students as I once felt toward newspaper readers—fratricidal.

Obviously, this isn't the ideal way to feel, but you might feel the same way after spending an entire semester emphasizing to students the need for discipline and precision in their writing, only to receive a final paper containing in the very first paragraph the sentence, "There is much at steak here." Even for an occasional meat-eater like myself, such stuff is hard to swallow.

Anyone who teaches could tell a similar tale. In fact, every occupational or professional group could cite incidents that call into doubt the mental prowess of its clients. For example, my wife, coordinator of the immunization program in a county health department, once asked a young woman attending a clinic if she was sexually active. "No," the woman replied, "I just lie there."

The problem occurs when this sort of thing stops seeming funny and becomes merely another piece of evidence that most people have lower IQs than the average household pet. In the course of our daily rounds, all of us have had the misfortune of running into service workers, from accountants and doctors to toll-takers and sales clerks, who seem to hate the public. Their professional manners consist of glumness, self-interest, and a cold, creepy contempt for those who depend on their help.

But you don't deserve to be treated contemptuously and neither do I (even if I am a school board member). Neither, I suspect, do our students. Is it really their fault that they don't read or write so well? Are they really to blame for their ignorance of history and their indifference to current events? Not when the American family has all the stability of a depressive who has skipped several doses of Prozac. Not when kids are encouraged by advertising and adult example to prowl the mall or watch unlimited television. Not when the culture at large puts a premium on consumption and leisure.

It is an unofficial but important part of my responsibilities as a school board member to listen to the concerns of parents about their children's teachers. Their stories, when they stop me in the supermarket parking lot or at the soccer field, are alarming. A 4th grade teacher who habitually ridicules a student for being quiet and shy. A middle school science teacher who returns tests late or not at all. A high school English teacher who reads *The Scarlet Letter* aloud to his class rather than trusting students to read it on their own. What all these little incidents have in common are teachers who despise, or at least don't nurture, the children placed in their care.

A contemporary ethical theorist with the apt name of Clifford Christians has argued that a society is only as good as its treatment of its most vulnerable members—the old, the sick, the poor, the disenfranchised. We might extend this list to include students, and not only those of younger age. One morning a couple of semesters ago, I was about to rip into a reporting class for being particularly unresponsive to my questions. From past experience, the students knew what was coming and dropped their eyes and slouched deeper into their seats. Then it hit me: I was alienating them. I can't remember whether our discussion of leads got any better after that, but I do know my teaching has.

Two widely recognized ethical principles undergird my approach to teaching now: reciprocity and universality. Reciprocity refers to treating other people as you would want to be treated yourself, while universality refers to acting as you would want other people to act in similar situations. These aren't hard principles to grasp, just to practice.

They are hard to practice for a variety of reasons: because surviving the daily battle seems to require armoring one's heart; because the educational culture as well as the culture at large emphasizes outcomes over process; because the classroom has become a kind of Salvation Army drop box for every pressing social problem; and because schools are rigidly hierarchical institutions, with each layer—students, teachers, administrators, school board members—tending to be contemptuous of the others.

Does this mean we should give up, that we should wave the white flag and surrender to the contempt syndrome? Never. If we can't learn to love, we can at least learn not to hate. And the first day of school can be today.

ⓘ7

GRAMMARAMA

If bad writing were a crime, most Americans would be under felony indictment. Students graduate from high school today unable to distinguish the difference between "its" and "it's," or "their" and "there," or "than" and "then." They confuse the functions of a comma with those of a period, and they haven't the least idea what a semicolon is for (no, it's not part of the human intestine). Their prose, if one can designate their often childish scribblings as such, is marred by misspellings, misusages, and outright barbarisms.

Is this a tragedy? Maybe not. Mr. Dooley, the immigrant Irish bartender created by Finley Peter Dunne to satirize America in the Gilded Age, once said, "When we Americans are through with th' English language, it will look as if it'd been run over by a musical comedy." It could be we just haven't gotten to the songs and funny scenes yet.

At the state university where I teach, other professors also complain about the inability of their students (the vast majority of them products of the public education system) to write well. My colleagues sigh that clear writing has become increasingly rare, a lost art, like scrimshaw or persiflage. We all wonder what will happen next and worry that whatever it is, it will represent a new kind of Dark Ages, when everyone will be living in a consumer cornucopia, but no one will be able to spell it.

The decline of writing parallels the rise of moral relativism, the attitude that anyone should be allowed to do anything as long as it doesn't hurt anyone else. It is an attitude that, for all its democratic virtues, has serious potential drawbacks. If the only accepted rules are those that are personally defined, if individual rights always trump shared responsibilities, then social organization begins to break down. The loss of coherence may even seep into writing and ultimately swamp it.

I don't mean to come off sounding like sour old Miss Mapes, my 5th grade teacher at Lakeside School back in 1961 and a stickler for rules. A slavish devotion to rules can actually interfere with expression. Thomas Jefferson, perhaps the greatest literary stylist in American political history, recognized that. When preparing his first State of the Union message, he sent a draft to James Madison for comment, asking his friend and fellow Virginian to pay special heed to the language: "Where strictness of grammar does not weaken expression, it should be attended to in complaisance to the purists of New England. But where by small grammatical negligences the energy of an idea is condensed, or a word stands for a sentence, I hold grammatical rigor in contempt."

Jefferson knew correct grammar and so could knowingly violate it to achieve a desired effect. Students lack this kind of pinpoint control over their writing. In a recent batch of papers, mine spelled Santa Claus as "Santa Clause," donor as "doner," and dilemma as "delima," used possessives without apostrophes, and wrote sentences without predicates. They didn't make these mistakes on purpose. They made them because they don't know any better. Whatever rules of writing they were once taught—and I assume they were taught some—they have pretty much forgotten. They blunder about the snow-white pages like early Arctic explorers searching with a broken compass in a blinding blizzard for a nonexistent route.

Whose fault is this? Many experts say it is at least partly television's. I might as well, too, and for all the obvious reasons: Television corrupts taste, promotes passivity, and privileges pictures over words. Also, the endless hours spent watching it could be better spent in reading and reflection—that is, absorbing the qualities of good writing, fixing them in one's mind. I myself learned grammar through some such process of literary osmosis. Reading can repair a lot of the damage done in the past by poor teachers or a student's own laziness and inattention.

Unfortunately, the reading material lying around the waiting room of life is often junk. Students grow up today inundated with print messages, but many of these are commercial in character and of little or no value as models of good writing. I'm convinced, for example, that one reason why student essays are so riddled with incomplete sentences is that advertising copy generally is. Scraps of language darkly glittering on glossy paper. A few simple, insidious phrases. Arranged in brief lines to catch the eyes. And, of course, selling something.

Overexposure to the fraudulent charm of commercial prose can condition students to think and write almost entirely in fragments. Perhaps even worse, though, is what they learn (or don't learn) about writing at school. If the notices they bring home in their backpacks are any indication, they are being subjected in class to all kinds of linguistic depravity.

From the high school comes a letter containing the sentence, "Selecting a class ring is a regarding choice," which, frankly, reads like it was written by someone who has no regard for language or logic. From the physical education department comes a letter that commits more errors than the butterfingered infield of a Little League team, including two in spelling, nine in punctuation, and four in tense agreement. And just when I'm saying to myself with relief, "Well, at least these people don't teach English," along comes a letter from an English teacher that refers to "youse," as in that favorite phrase of mobster movies, "youse guys."

I think it isn't asking too much that teachers at all grade levels and in all disciplines be literate. Until they are, they will embarrass themselves and their profession, as well as disserve their students. Teachers' unions, school boards, and colleges of education need to acknowledge that a problem exists here and do something to solve it. For the colleges, this may mean tighter admission standards and a tougher curriculum, while for the unions and school boards, it may mean better hiring practices, more staff development, and, in cases of recalcitrant teachers, excommunication.

As for students, they should write, write, write, and read, read, read (the New York State Board of Regents recently recommended that high schoolers read twenty-five books a year). All teachers, no matter what their subject areas, should regularly assign writing and then collect and critique the assignments, not just put a check on them. Moreover, spelling and grammar should count. This would emphasize to students that abiding by certain rules is as helpful in writing as it is in games and sports. Students wouldn't disobey the rules when playing tennis or Nintendo. Why should writing, a far more complicated and delicate act, be any different?

Society has a right to expect that the graduates of its public schools will be able to construct a grammatical sentence. The graduates themselves have a right to the power inherent in full literacy. In the end, democracy isn't about doing your own thing. It is about giving people the opportunity and the tools—including the writing tools—to make their voices heard.

18

X-THICS

You ought to feel sorry for me. I teach an undergraduate course in journalism ethics at a time when ethics seems to matter less and less in the conduct of professional journalists. My students and I want to believe that journalism is, in protoinvestigative reporter Jacob Riis's stirring phrase, "the noblest of all callings," but then we glance at a newspaper or flip on a TV and are reminded once again that it just isn't so.

The other day I flipped on MSNBC—a big mistake, it turned out, given my already fragile state of mind. Who should be guest-hosting one of the blab-a-thons that pass for insightful news coverage on the channel but Mike Barnicle. This is the same Mike Barnicle who resigned in disgrace from the *Boston Globe* in 1998 after evidence mounted that he plagiarized items and fabricated sources and quotes for his popular column.

As I stared at his mug, with the large, lumpy features of a football player from the pre-face-mask era, I kept wondering, What's this miscreant doing holding forth on TV? For that matter, what's he doing writing a regular column for the *New York Daily News*? I always thought that there was no room in journalism for liars and thieves. The Society of Professional Journalists' Code of Ethics plainly states, "Deliberate distortion is never permissible," as well as commands, "Never plagiarize." And yet here was Barnicle, who had broken these precepts (or at least mangled them pretty badly), posing with the connivance of MSNBC as a model journalist. I felt like throwing up.

There is no shortage of journalistic codes of ethics, just of ethical journalism. Codes say journalists should avoid pandering to lurid curiosity, but news organizations deliver frequent jolts of sex, blood, and scandal to capture public attention. Codes say journalists should identify sources whenever feasible, but even routine political stories now contain anonymous quotes. Codes say journalists should distinguish between news and advertising, but a profits-above-all mentality has eroded the line between the two. Codes say journalists should show compassion for people affected by tragedy or grief, but scoop-hungry reporters trample privacy and other rights underfoot in their mad rush to be first with the latest.

If ethics has any practical purpose in newsrooms today, it is as silver polish for tarnished news judgments. The *Arizona Republic* provides a particularly grisly example of what I mean. This past summer a Phoenix man committed suicide by lying down on a conveyor belt and feeding himself into a wood chipper. To add to the horror of the incident, he tried to drag his fiancée in after him. Metro team leader Bill Hart assured readers in an editorial note that he and his staff wrestled all day with the question of whether this was news or "a titillating grostequerie disguised as news." Guess what they decided? The story ran on the front of the metro section.

The point journalists don't seem to get—perhaps because they don't want to get it—is that wrestling with an ethical decision isn't the same as actually reaching an ethical decision. At a minimum, ethics requires that you be able to publicly justify a decision on the basis of a recognized ethical principle. Hart never said why the bizarre suicide was something readers needed to know, though he did mention that an earlier story about a man who killed himself by jumping into a wood chipper was the No. 1 pick on the paper's website.

This kind of market-driven coverage makes teaching journalism ethics increasingly difficult. When my students look around, what do they see? Editors mouthing moral platitudes while publishing slimy garbage. Reporters acting without restraint and being rewarded for it. News organizations claiming to preserve freedom, but joining the herd of corporate behemoths crashing about the culture. Why should students take journalism ethics seriously? No one else apparently does.

Just recently, a Gallup poll found that public confidence in the press is at a fifteen-year low. Journalists always seem somewhat surprised when surveys reveal that the public doesn't like or trust them. But how could it be otherwise? The press has shown about as much regard for ethics as have the wrongdoers it so eagerly exposes—the president who lies under oath, the civil rights leader who fathers a child out of wedlock, the sports hero who batters his girlfriend, the movie star who snorts coke. Rather than help refurbish our shabby institutions, journalists have taken up residence in a decayed building on the same crumbling block.

These are disillusioning times, and we unlucky few who teach journalism ethics must find ways to overcome our students' premature cynicism. We can draw on the moral philosophies of Aristotle, Immanuel Kant, and John Stuart Mill. We can explore questions of moral responsibility via case studies. We can cite the moral courage of great journalists of the past: Ida B. Wells, the black "Princess of the Press," who investigated Southern lynchings at the risk of her very life, or Heywood Broun, who used his column in the old *New York World* to plead for Sacco and Vanzetti over publisher Ralph Pulitzer's objections.

In the end, though, it may not matter what happens in the classroom if newsrooms continue to practice no-fault ethics. I often worry that when my students graduate into the fast and furious world of journalism, they will quickly forget Aristotle and the rest and succumb to the profession's ethical chaos. The mere prospect of that ought to be enough to make you feel sorry not just for me, but for us all.

⑲

ADVICE TO GRADUATES

When I graduated from high school in 1969, my parents gave me a dictionary as a graduation gift. I know what you're thinking: What a crappy gift! I thought so, too, then, but I was wrong. Just how wrong? Despite now having spell check on my computer, I still rely on that old dictionary, whose full title is *The Random House Dictionary of the English Language*, the Unabridged Edition. Almost two thousand closely printed pages long, the dictionary is about as thick as a cinder block when closed and about as wide as the wingspan of a gull when open. It lies open on my writing table at this very moment, like a gull gliding on a gracious wind.

My mom and dad, who never went beyond high school, gave me the dictionary in the poignant belief that it would somehow ease the mental trauma of reading college textbooks and writing college term papers. Considering the lackluster grades I got in college, it didn't work nearly as well as they had intended. But, like most parental gifts, the dictionary has grown in value over the years. As I have passed ("lumbered" might be a better word) through the various stages of my career, from graduate student to journalist to professor to author, the dictionary has usually been just an arm's length away, my fat, faithful sidekick on a journey with few maps.

Why should you care? What can my beat-up old dictionary, its faded cloth cover bent at the corners like a piece of junk metal, possibly do for you graduates? As a reference book, not much, since it is hopelessly out of date, listing Richard Nixon as the current U.S. president. But as a metaphor, a symbol of how to approach life after high school, the dictionary may offer some useful lessons.

Lesson #1: The best gifts sometimes come in the worst wrapping. In many fairy tales, a crooked little man gives a youth a seemingly insignificant item—a bean, a pebble—that turns out to possess magic powers. Or, rather, the item allows the youth to discover hitherto unsuspected powers in him- or herself: courage, ingenuity, perseverance. With the help of a mere bean, Jack became a giant-killer; with the help of a dictionary, I became an author. All of us encounter somewhere in our lives a crooked little man, or his equivalent, with a magic bean resting in his horny palm. The trick is to be alert enough to recognize what a wonderful gift he is holding out to us and to be daring enough to take it.

Lesson #2: Knowledge is less important, ultimately, than the ability to acquire it. Keep a dictionary handy. Look things up. Be curious. "The business of life," essayist Jonathan Rosen said, "is not to know, but to learn." Investigative reporter I. F. Stone was a lifelong learner. When he was forced to retire from journalism in 1971 because of ill health, Stone still had one last story to tell. A student of history and philosophy, as well as a committed civil libertarian, he had long been haunted by the death of Socrates. In 399 B.C. a jury of five hundred Athenians had tried Socrates for corrupting the youth of their city with his teachings. Found guilty and condemned to die, Socrates had drunk a cup of hemlock. Stone was intrigued by the paradox of Athens, the cradle of democracy, executing its most outspoken citizen and greatest thinker.

So he probed the case, just as he had probed the conduct of the Vietnam War and the underground testing of nuclear weapons when he was a reporter. What he found to his frustration was that the scholarly authorities on ancient Greece contradicted each other. But rather than give up, Stone learned classical Greek in order to be able to examine the evidence for himself. The fruit of his labor is a book titled *The Trial of Socrates*, published in 1980, and something more: the inspiring example of a man who couldn't be kept from exploring new areas by the barriers of illness, age, or language. And neither should you. In a sense, you shouldn't ever graduate, but should remain a student for life, with the world your happily cluttered desk.

Lesson #3, the last lesson: Treasure certain words, bright, hopeful words, such as freedom, justice, and peace. Unfortunately, we live in an age where bright words are often used to camouflage dark missions, where governments uproot and terrorize populations and call it "peace-keeping," or corporations smash trees and pave over meadows and call it "development." Call things by their true names, and if you don't know their true names, ask someone who does. Don't be the passive victim of words; be their kung fu master. And when on your path to mastery, you find a word whose promised meaning moves you, a word like kindness or community, inscribe it on your heart and define it by your deeds.

I can't remember who spoke at my high school graduation thirty-three years ago or what the speaker said, and soon you won't remember what I said here today either. But before you forget, realize at least this, that there aren't enough words in my dictionary, as big as it is, for all the good things I wish you, starting with love and ending with happiness and including a handful of magic beans.

20

OFF TO SEE THE WIZARD

What defines somebody as educated? Is it getting a certain score on a standardized test? Is it passing through a prescribed curriculum? Is it being employable after graduation? If you listen to politicians and educational bureaucrats, you would probably think so. But who in his or her right mind wants to listen to politicians and bureaucrats? We need a better source of guidance in such important matters, and I nominate *The Wizard of Oz*—the Judy Garland movie, of course, not the original L. Frank Baum book.

It is my theory, based on almost yearly viewing of the movie since I was a kid, that the four companions who skip arm in arm down the Yellow Brick Road each represents a different essential aspect or goal of education. When you add what the Scarecrow wants (brains) to what the Tin Man wants (a heart) to what the Lion wants (courage) to what Dorothy wants (a home), you end up with a fully educated person. There is even a kind of graduation ceremony near the end of the movie during which the Wizard hands out awards and honors: a diploma to the Scarecrow, a heart-shaped watch to the Tin Man, and so on.

Although brainless, the Scarecrow is still somehow smart enough to recognize the value of having brains. He complains when he first meets Dorothy about the crows that come from miles around to eat in his field.

89

"Oh," he moans, "I'm a failure because I haven't got a brain." But as useful as a brain would be in helping him do his job, that isn't the only reason he wants one. He also wants a brain so he can experience the joy of understanding. As he sings: "Gosh, it would be awful pleasin'/to reason out the reason/For things I can't explain."

The Scarecrow reminds us that the real purpose of education isn't so much to prepare students to make a living as to prepare them to make a life. Today, though, it increasingly seems that the only purpose of education is to prepare students to take tests—diagnostic tests, achievement tests, aptitude tests, state tests. What teacher wouldn't love to have a student who joyfully sings and dances, as the Scarecrow does, about "a chance of getting some brains"? But what student will feel much like singing and dancing if education becomes evermore synonymous with high-stakes testing? You don't have to be a wizard to see the threat to the joy of understanding in that.

Even if it were true that harder and more frequent tests lead to bigger and better brains, I'm not sure that braininess should be considered the defining characteristic of an educated person. Brains can crack the genetic code of a virus, but can they be trusted to use such fearful knowledge only for good? Brains can invent new forms of work and travel and communication, but can they alone determine what is worth doing, or seeing, or saying? Aristotle pointed out long ago something that we ourselves always seem in danger of forgetting. "Educating the mind," he observed, "without educating the heart is no education at all."

Which brings us to our hollow-chested friend, the Tin Man. Although the Wizard warns him, "Hearts will never be practical until they can be made unbreakable," he wants one anyway. Why? Because he is "presumin'" that he could be "kind-a human" if he "only had a heart." Having a brain buzzing with ideas and reasons is a fine thing, just not everything. A heart capable of registering the great emotions—love, devotion, pity—is also necessary.

Contemporary culture glamorizes technology and treats the human as outdated and inefficient, something to be overcome rather than respected. We are so dazzled by technological breakthroughs that we fail to notice this antihuman ideology, this weird form of self-alienation fostered and circulated by the very media that most profit from it. When we aren't hunkered down in front of our satellite TV, we are hunkered

down in front of our PC; when we aren't answering our pager, we are answering our cell phone; when we aren't listening to a CD, we are watching a DVD. We spend larger and larger amounts of time attached to ma-
chines of one sort or another. Despite the freedom that new
technologies are supposed to afford us, we seem, with each technological advance, to become more, not less, robotic, turning ourselves into tin
men—and women.

Few of us are likely to suddenly abandon our pagers and CD burners
and Palm Pilots and go back to the garden. The problem, therefore, is
how to keep the heart, traditionally seen as the seat not only of feeling,
but also of judgment and moral wisdom, from getting lost in the clutter
at the bottom of our cultural closet. Some schools try through so-called
"character education," which draws on the ethos of the world's major re-
ligions and the sayings of standard philosophers and writers. But can a
daily quote from Confucius, or Abraham Lincoln, or Martin Luther
King reverse the numbing effects of watching all those ass-shaking MTV
videos or of playing all those ass-kicking video games? I tend to doubt it.

So what will? Perhaps introducing students to the plight of child soldiers and child workers around the world. If students can't relate too
well to the teachings of ancient philosophers, perhaps they can relate
better to the suffering of others their own age, to the more than
200,000 children, some as young as six, recruited to serve as soldiers in
government and rebel armies. Or to the 250 million children between
the ages of five and fourteen forced to work for a living. The figures
are enough to break your heart—two million children killed in wars
during the past decade, 50–60 million working in hazardous conditions—
but sometimes, as the Tin Man himself might say, the heart must break
in order to grow.

It would require courage, the trait the Lion so desperately wants, to
teach or even learn such stuff. For once students realize with their
hearts as well as their heads that woven into trendy GAP clothes or
molded into the latest Air Jordans is the agony of children who work
fourteen-hour days in sweatshops, no trip to the mall will ever be the
same careless fun again. The realization goes against the whole commercial flow of our culture, which submerges the actual, often intoler-
able conditions of production beneath bright, giddy waves of advertising. And yet if education means anything, shouldn't it mean teaching

students to be morally and intellectually courageous, to question the culture's frenzied faith in materialism and stake their identities on something more substantial than a bunch of brand names?

"Life," writer Anais Nin said, "shrinks or expands in proportion to one's courage." School life is, by this measure, a dried-up, shrunken thing. In fact, schools as now constituted seem primarily designed to promote not courage or curiosity among students, but passiveness and conformity. A person with a somewhat skeptical turn of mind might even see character education, with its emphasis on old-fashioned virtues like responsibility and respect, as a device to render students more obedient to authority. Not that there aren't plenty of such devices already, from dress codes and drug tests to metal detectors at the doors and armed guards and surveillance cameras in the halls. The atmosphere at many schools, particularly many high schools, doesn't come close to addressing what may be students' greatest need: connection and community, a sense of belonging. Rather, the atmosphere adds to the aching emptiness, like horrible old Miss Gulch trying to take away Toto, Dorothy's one friend.

Dorothy is an orphan living on a dreary Kansas farm with her Aunt Em and Uncle Henry. Some years ago, sociologist Peter Berger wrote a book called *The Homeless Mind* whose central thesis was that modern society has left most of its members feeling like orphans. Berger noted that the traditions and affiliations—familial, occupational, ethnic, religious—from which people once drew a sense of belonging have been destroyed or degraded by the forces of modernization, with the result that the world has become a colder, darker, lonelier place. Recent statistics suggest that it is especially cold and dark and lonely for young people. One government survey found, for example, that nearly three million Americans from ages twelve to seventeen considered suicide in 2000 and that more than a third of those actually tried to kill themselves.

As Dorothy discovers, you can go over the rainbow and still not escape your troubles, still not feel understood or appreciated by others. The anxieties that the poor girl suffered in black-and-white Kansas take even more terrifying form after she thumps down in the rockin' psychedelic Land of Oz. She must now contend with a wicked witch, crabby talking trees, and winged monkeys. No wonder she wants to get back home.

I often hear teachers and school administrators complaining about how tough their job has become. They say academic standards have never been so strict, or students so needy, or parents so uninvolved. They may be right, too. Their situation may be unfair, though I can't help wondering whether they couldn't use a little of the Wizard in them. The Wizard is mostly blather, a con man with no special powers beyond his remarkable gift for obfuscation. Nonetheless, he sets Dorothy and her friends a task—"Bring me the broomstick of the Witch of the West!"—and much to their own surprise, they accomplish it. School should be more like that. Students should cross the threshold of a challenge and find on the other side, after a series of symbolic adventures, brains and heart and courage. It seems to me the only way we'll ever get home again.

ABOUT THE AUTHOR

Howard Good (B.A., Bard College; M.A., University of Iowa; Ph.D., University of Michigan) has served six years on the Highland (N.Y.) school board, the last three as president. He is also vice president of the Ulster County School Boards Association. His commentaries on education have appeared in such national publications as *American School Board Journal, Education Week*, and *Teacher Magazine*. A professor of journalism at SUNY New Paltz, he has written eight books, including *Girl Reporter* and *The Drunken Journalist*, and edited a volume of essays titled *Desperately Seeking Ethics: A Guide to Media Conduct*. His book-in-progress, *The Theory of Oz: Rediscovering the Aims of Education*, will be published by ScarecrowEducation.